RESTAURANT
RESTAURANT

Classic FRENCH CUISINE

Edited by Rosemary Moon

TIGER BOOKS INTERNATIONAL
LONDON

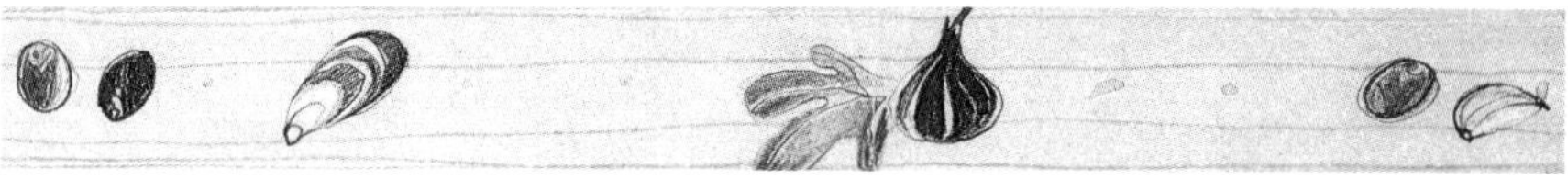

ILLUSTRATIONS BY
CAMILLA SOPWITH AND LAWRIE TAYLOR

CLB 4367
This edition published 1995 by
Tiger Books International PLC, Twickenham

Typeset by SX Composing, Rayleigh, Essex

Printed and bound in South Africa
ISBN 1-85501-620-6

CONTENTS

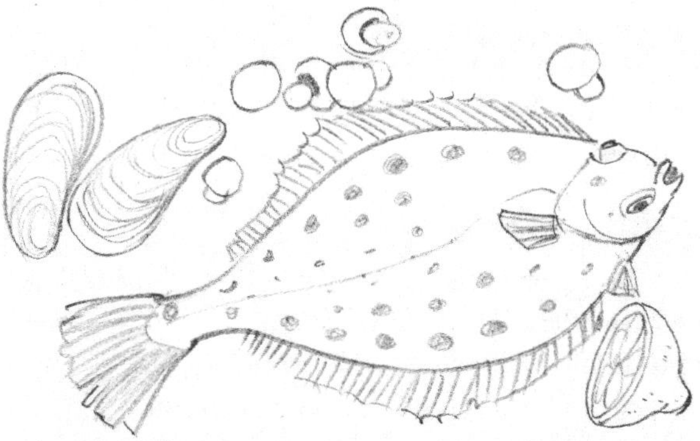

INTRODUCTION

What makes France the greatest nation of food lovers and cooks, the land of the premier cuisine of the world? The answer is perfectly simple – the French know and care about their food.

The Mediterranean Effect

I have a theory that the Mediterranean is a big influence on the general attitude of people towards food. Perhaps it is because the countries which border the Mediterranean all enjoy long hot summers and people have to adapt their life-styles to the heat of the day if they are to work, day in and day out, in such high temperatures. This means that life is taken at a more leisurely pace than in other, cooler climates; a good lunch might be enjoyed before a rest from the mid-day sun, then more work is undertaken before supper or dinner, served late in the cool of the evening. Indeed lunch is still a big meal, if not the main meal, of the day in France – I have enjoyed several four course mid-day meals in office dining rooms!

No Friday Night Supermarket Panic!

The French know and understand their food and they are proud of it. If a meal takes a long time to prepare, so much the better – good food is more likely to be demanding on the cook or the shopper than a hurriedly put together and quickly forgotten snack. That isn't to say that good food must always take hours to prepare but, if a meal is to be a simple celebration of fine ingredients, then time would have to be spent in selection and shopping for that meal. A frantic trip around the supermarket on a Friday night, buying everything that is to be consumed by the household until the following Friday, will not allow for the loving preparation of meals that will satisfy and stimulate the family.

All Great Traditions Must Adapt

Perhaps, because I rather idolise the cooking of France and the dedication of the average Frenchman to the pleasures of the table, I am more than a little reluctant to acknowledge that attitudes towards food might be changing, even in the world centre of fine cuisine. I have no doubt at all that things are changing in the cities, and that convenience foods are playing a larger and larger part in many homes where both parents work and there is a family to feed daily, and not that much time in which to do it. One has to hope that the convenience foods are of a high standard – but I am sure that they don't compare with home cooked food. The most vital ingredient in any dish is love and there's no way that the average food manufacturer can reproduce the tastes and textures achievable by someone cooking for family or friends.

What makes the country cookery of France so outstanding is that, through a dedication to the best foods available locally, the French have evolved a cuisine which is relatively simple and requires little in the way of modern kitchen wizardry to produce mouth-watering dishes.

Haute Cuisine and Cuisine Bourgeois

Both have their place but might become muddled in people's

minds, especially if they think that all French cuisine is haute cuisine. *Haute cuisine* is the stuff of banquets, of fine city restaurants, large chateaux and the ultimate dedication of life to the enjoyment of food and wine. It was a way of life for many in the late nineteenth and early twentieth centuries but few of us can stand such indulgence now, on our bank accounts, our hearts or our waistlines!

Such fine living is not the benchmark for the vast majority of French people – they derive their reputation for wonderful food through their regional and family inheritances of an outstanding appreciation of local ingredients, the ability to shop well and the tried and tested recipes of the generations that preceded them. It is this more simple culinary heritage, one which influences the vast majority of the French people, that truly earns France its reputation as the culinary centre of the world.

From Seaside Bistro to Transport Café

The most wonderful thing to me about food in France today is that there is no snobbery attached to it. Everyone demands good food – the transport café frequented by long distance lorry drivers would serve food undreamed of on journeys on major roads in other countries. The French drivers simply would not return to a restaurant serving poor quality convenience food. The menu might include a limited selection of dishes but they are usually freshly prepared by skilled cooks producing honest food for the appreciation and enjoyment of others. The most outwardly un-inspiring restaurant in a small village or country town will probably serve delightful meals at really affordable prices. And, if you don't want to cook yourself, where better to enjoy fresh seafood than at a harbour-side bistro?

Of course there are exclusive restaurants throughout France, many of them constantly busy. But who pays the inflated prices which these establishments charge? You are more likely to find them full of tourists if close to the fashionable resorts of the south, or expense account executives mingling with celebrities at chic restaurants in busy cities.

Regional Country Cooking

So many books have now been published on regional French cookery that it is easy to see how important this country cooking is to the cuisine of France. Of course there are recipes common throughout the country, but there are also regional variations and specialities. Many areas cook extensively with wine – indeed it is really impossible to divorce food from wine when taking an overview of the French cuisine. The use of wine is influenced by its voluminous production – fine wines are produced virtually throughout the country with the exception of Normandy and Brittany, where cider making is of greater importance. The local wine is used for many native dishes – it has the right characteristics to mix with the local produce – why marinade native beef in a wine from a vineyard which is hundreds of kilometres away? No, the grape and the meat of the area will be made for each other, complementary ingredients for wonderful dishes.

Perhaps the current interest in French cookery stems from the fashion for more comforting foods – the return of the nursery pudding, and rich warming casseroles with hearty accompaniments? The French have always, in their regional dishes, managed to produce really satisfying fare from even the cheapest and toughest cuts of meat, cooking them slowly with plenty of vegetables, herbs and seasonings. This skill came through necessity in the days when the rich used only the best from any carcass and left the scraps for the servants and others to feed on. Time in those days was cheap – for many of us it is now a luxury.

The Culinary Regions of France

There are twelve principal culinary areas, although I sometimes get the feeling when I am in France that the district in which people live is almost of the same importance as the region, but it is by the regions that most of us associate wines and foods.

What is grown and farmed locally will greatly influence the food of the region. Perhaps one of the best examples of this is the cooking of Normandy, which can be very rich as it is an area of dairy farming, of milk, cheese, butter and cream production. The shellfish found along the coast is also widely used and the overall richness of the food is offset by the extensive use of apples in both sweet and savoury dishes, for this is also the land of cider production. That said, Calvados, the apple brandy of the region, may easily obliterate all memories of what has gone before if served by too generous a host!

Every Region has its Own Speciality

I have already mentioned many of the speciality foods of Normandy. Others include the lambs which feed on the coastal salt marshes and a salad combining the best of all the local ingredients, apples, shell fish and cheeses; a Salade Normande.

Oysters & Artichokes

Brittany juts out into the Atlantic Ocean and supports a very important fishing industry. Oysters, lobsters and salt cod are all specialities of Brittany, as are the huge globe artichokes and cauliflowers that are the pride of the region.

Where the north coast adjoins Normandy the Bretons share with their neighbours a love of *pré-salé* salt marsh lamb. Brittany is also a land of crêpes and galettes, variations on a pancake theme which were eaten as staple foods when Brittany was isolated and unable to produce enough wheat for bread. Crêpes are now almost a fast food, available from stalls and small vans in market places. As to my favourite Breton food, after the globe artichokes which I adore – well, it's the Gâteau Breton, a very buttery cake to be eaten by itself or with stewed fruits or mousses – delicious!

The Loire, Historical Nursery of France

The Loire Valley is rich and fertile, producing top quality greengrocery. The Loire has been the nursery for many new fruits and vegetables introduced to France by explorers and travelling monarchs. King Charles VIII introduced Italian gardeners to Amboise, his Loire chateau, and they grew lettuces and peas. Indeed, there is a recipe for Petits Pois à la Française, where peas are actually cooked with shredded lettuce – it's different, delicious and well worth trying! Peaches, now one of the best and most prolific fruits in France, were also established in the Loire Valley and are extensively grown to this day, along with apricots, melons and pears.

Quenelles – a Fish Speciality

The Loire provides wonderful river fish – pike are still plentiful and Quenelles au Beurre Blanc, light spoonfuls of pike, poached and served in butter sauce, is a traditional dish of the Loire.

A Cathedral, Pâtés and a Tradition of Baking

These are the claims to fame of Chartres, the famous cathedral city in the north of the Loire region. When the monks were building the cathedral much of the surrounding land was cleared to provide building materials and this was then planted with wheat. The area, Beauce, became known as the granary of France. Chartres is also famed for its game pâtés – less acceptable is the local liking for lark pâté, something which I have no intention of trying.

Prunes, Oysters & Truffles

What a mixture! These foods all come from the South West, a region of which I have especially happy memories, for it was here that I first tasted French food prepared in a French home. In my early teens I set off on a concert tour of France with the local youth orchestra (in which I played the trumpet!). Our conductor had friends in a tiny village and some eighty teenagers descended to give the first concert in the village church this century! Almost every house in the village had at least one English person staying there and, before the concert, we all ate cassoulet *en famille* in the village square. Two days that triggered my life-long love of French food and customs!

A Profusion of Fish

The rivers of the South West offer excellent fish but it is the Atlantic coast that has established the reputation of the area for fine oysters, scallops and Dublin Bay prawns (scampi). The oyster industry is centered on Arcachon, south of Bordeaux, where a huge, shallow bay provides an excellent breeding ground. The oysters take three years to reach a saleable size – a massive investment for the oyster farmers. Unfortunately, the farming yields slightly less flavoursome oysters than those able to grow in the wild. The Bordelaise – the people of Bordeaux – often eat tiny sausages with their oysters (and, of course, they drink white wine with them!) which helps to give a little more flavour. Oysters raised at Marennes, north of Bordeaux, have more flavour and a quite distinctive greenish colour – both characteristics are due to the algae present in the oyster beds.

Pruneaux d'Agen – the Finest Prunes in the World

The town of Agen on the Garonne is the centre of the plum

growing area which produces the *pruneaux d'Agen*, huge moist prunes that I believe are the finest in the world. Most of the growers have their own drying ovens and there is a heady sweetness in the air when the plums are being dried in late September.

The Secret of the Oak Woods

Truffles are a type of edible fungus and the most famous truffle region in France is around Périgord and Quercy, where the highly prized black truffle is in season from November to March. They grow underground on the roots of oak trees and are found by truffle hunters with pigs or dogs to help them – it is said that pigs are more efficient at hunting but dogs are easier to discipline once a truffle has been located! Most truffles are canned, which prolongs their season but lessens their flavour. Only a slice or two is required to flavour any dish as they can be somewhat pungent.

The Pyrenees & Gascony – a Spanish Influence

This region is tucked away on the Spanish border and is greatly influenced by Spain. Peppers and olives are used extensively and salt cod is popular – Brandade de Morue, a creamy paste of the preserved fish is a local speciality.

Exotic Fish & Air-Dried Hams

The Basque fishermen were great whalers but now the catch is mainly tuna, swordfish, sardines and anchovies. The Basque passion for spicy seasoning is reflected in their fish cookery – a local recipe for swordfish cooked with green peppercorns is included in the chapter on fish and seafood.

Named after the principal town of the region, jambons de Bayonne are air-dried and then usually eaten raw, very thinly sliced. The hams have been renowned since the Middle Ages and much of the special flavour comes from Espelette, the red peppers with which the hams are rubbed during curing. In some rural areas the number of hams hanging up to dry still gives an indication of the wealth of the household – you need to be able to afford the pigs in the first place!

Pickled in Armagnac!

Gascony adjoins the South Western region of France, sharing a common border through the Armagnac producing country. Much of the cooking of the area reflects an ancient tradition of food preservation, setting aside a store for consumption during the long, hard days of winter. Luxurious as fruits in Armagnac sounds to us, the tradition arose through the need to preserve the fruits for the winter months.

Confit – the Fat of the Land?

Confit is a method of preserving meats and poultry by salting and then cooking with fat. Goose fat is the most commonly used, and there are many geese in this area! The meat is usually preserved in large pieces cooked very slowly, totally covered in fat, until it is almost melting. Once cold the meat is covered in more melted fat, and then the *confit* is stored – it will keep for several months in the refrigerator.

Eat *confit* hot in a simple dish of beans or vegetables, frying it in its own fat until crispy. It may also be eaten cold in salads and is considered to be one of the great delicacies of France.

Languedoc – Land of Roquefort, Garlic & Salt

Languedoc is the central southern region of France. Its main crop is wine and one department, the Hérault, produces one fifth of the total wine of France! However, the three most important foods of the area are Roquefort, garlic and salt.

Roquefort, a pungent blue ewes' milk cheese, is the only cheese in France to have its own *appèllation controllé*. It is matured for three months in the same limestone caves that have been used since 1411. It is now necessary to import sheep's milk from elsewhere to achieve a production of more than 12 million kilos a year.

Almost all the salt used in France is produced from the Salins du Midi, huge salt water lakes in the Camargue. Most chefs and cooks prefer sea or rock salt for cooking so it is no wonder that the French value this naturally produced seasoning.

Languedoc produces the best garlic in France. Garlic stalls are found in every market and many towns and villages have annual garlic fairs. Vampires are seldom seen in this area! Garlic is supposed to be good for you but too much may ruin your social life! Remember that sometimes just rubbing a cut clove around a salad bowl or over the surface of an ingredient will give all the flavour that is required.

Provençe – A Little Province of Italy?

The Italian influence is clearly to be seen in the food of Provençe, so named as it was once a province of the Roman Empire. Tomatoes, garlic, herbs in plenty, olives, onions and anchovies combine with fish, vegetables and meat to offer a very varied, well flavoured cuisine.

Olives & Olive Oil – a Provençal Way of Life

Provençe is *the* main olive producing area of France. Black olives are merely green olives that have been left to ripen for longer on the trees but both are virtually inedible if eaten straight after picking. The olives have to be matured in lye, a strong alkaline solution, before they are ready for eating. The best are then packed in olive oil for sale.

Olive oil has become one of the most fashionable ingredients in contemporary cookery and whole books have been written on the subject. Virgin and Extra Virgin oils, the purest varieties, are now easily produced and are affordable thanks to the introduction of centrifugal presses. A good olive oil, in my opinion, has a peppery finish and a good green colour.

Franche-Comté & the Alps

This region borders both Italy and Switzerland and is guarded by Mont Blanc. It is a mountainous region and home to some of the best wild mushrooms, walnuts and game in France.

Wild mushrooms are the perfect accompaniment to game and, interestingly enough, often grow in good hunting areas. Care should be taken if you are a wild mushroom hunter – some are just not as edible as they look! In France most markets have a good selection of the mushrooms in season and there is little necessity to find your own if you are not skilled in fungus recognition! It simply is not worth taking any risks as some varieties are deadly.

The fresh crop of walnuts each autumn is an indication that winter is drawing in. Walnut oil is a delicious ingredient of salad dressings for special foods – I love it on avocados. It has helped to establish the walnut as a major crop – they were often grown as a secondary crop to supplement an income derived from vines, or vegetables. Walnuts are now valued for themselves, and justly so.

The French are great hunters and shooters and many game birds have to be farmed to ensure a regular supply for the table. Wild deer, rabbits and hare are common to this area and are hunted, as are small birds – a practice which I cannot condone.

Alsace-Lorraine, Home to Quiche and the Best Foie Gras

On a recent visit to Lorraine I was wondering what the locals ate apart from quiche! The answer was soft cheese and the most delicious hams and sausages, many of which clearly show a German influence.

Of course quiche is the best known dish of the region but the finest *foie gras* in France is also produced here.

Force-Feeding – a Natural Inclination

The Romans used to force-feed geese on figs to enlarge their livers and produce *foie gras* – the French now achieve the same result by feeding with maize. The average person, and especially a non-foody, would condemn this as barbaric but, although I have never actually seen the feeding done myself, except on the TV, various authorities have written that the geese actually seem to enjoy the feeding. It is true that geese are greedy and that they have always binged, especially before migration, so force-feeding is an extension of a natural tendency.

Foie Gras – *the* Delicacy

Throughout France *foie gras* is the gourmets delight. Buying it is really a matter of luck as even the most experienced eye cannot detect which liver will dissolve away to a pan full of little more than juices when cooked for just a moment too long. Fresh is best, but colour is no guide to quality as the livers vary from pink to a yellow ochre. The livers should be even in colour and cooked very lightly with next to no seasonings, allowing the delicate, slightly sweet flavour to dominate. Perhaps the easiest and best way to eat foie gras is with a slice of warm brioche, washed down with a glass of Sauternes or Champagne.

Champagne & the North

The cooking of this area is really very different to that of the rest of France, showing Belgian influence in the use of beer and an abundance of endive or chicory. Stews elsewhere are cooked in local wine, here carbonnades are popular, with the beef cooked in strong dark ale.

Chicory is often roasted with just a little onion, salt and pepper – I love it prepared like this as much of the bitter flavour, so strong in salads, is lost during cooking. Chicory is affordable in France – in England it is such a luxury – and it is always on my French shopping list! Vegetables are of prime importance to farmers in Champagne, and root vegetables in particular. It is one of the potato growing areas and the French have a great tradition of producing tasty potatoes – those grown particularly for salads are amongst my favourites.

Of course, the main crop of Champagne is fizzy . . .

Little & Large in the Centre of France

The Central region of France is a vast mountainous area containing the Massif Central and the Auvergne, an area famed for its excellent blue cheeses. It is home to the Limousin cattle, which produce prime beef and veal. At the other end of the scale, it is also an area producing a great number of frogs – what happens to their bodies is a mystery to me as one is only ever offered the legs!

The cabbage is the symbol of the Auvergne and it is widely used in the cooking of the area. Cabbage soup is a regional speciality and the vegetable is often added to casseroles or baked with small cuts of meat, especially pork.

My first memories of the Central region are of Vichy, an elegant spa town producing the famous water. I have played my trumpet in the opera house and it was in Vichy that I first tasted a proper vinaigrette – it was wonderful!

Last But Not Least

The region of Burgundy and the Lyonnais may be last on my list but it is the centre of many of the great food trades of France and, of course, it is home to one of the greatest wine traditions of the world. Lyon is the centre of the French charcuterie trade. The Lyonnais are also great lovers of chocolate and chestnuts, of prime quality around Lyon, which are often combined in sumptuous desserts. Snails, which are really an excuse for garlic butter in my opinion, are prized in Burgundy and *Escargot Bourguignon*, which are rather larger than other varieties of snail, are much prized. The cardoon, a relatively unknown vegetable outside France, looking like celery and having a flavour between a Jerusalem artichoke and fennel, is also grown here and is best braised slowly over a low heat.

The Home of Coq au Vin

Poultry is very popular in Burgundy and Coq au Vin, one of the greatest dishes of France, originates from here. Such a simple dish always sounds so impressive yet all that is required, as for so much French cookery, is good ingredients in prime condition. Beef cooked in the red wine of the region, Beef Bourguignon, is also internationally acclaimed.

The Centre of the World's Mustard Trade

Dijon, a relatively small town in the north of the region, produces over half the mustard consumed in the world! French mustard is considerably milder than English and is used extensively with rabbit and also with kidneys – recipes for both are included in this book.

From even such a brief introduction to the culinary regions of France, you will begin to understand how deeply food is associated with French traditions. Many monasteries and religious centres developed cheeses and liqueurs, and experimented with spices and ingredients brought from abroad by explorers. Combinations of new ingredients and traditional foods grown in France led to a development of the French cuisine which, to this day, just hasn't stopped. Great traditions only survive in a healthy state if they are able to change and adapt and French cooking has certainly done that! I have even included some new recipes in this book that I am certain are the classic French dishes of tomorrow!

The Vineyard of the World

Despite the huge variety of foods produced in France only 35 per cent of the land is arable, (24 per cent is pasture or grazing for animals) and as few as 7 per cent of the population are employed in agriculture. Included in the arable lands are the vineyards, which cover about 3.2 million acres and produce around 7 billion litres (1.8 billion gallons) of wine a year, making France and Italy jointly the largest wine producers in the world. France alone produces around one quarter of the world's wine.

I firmly believe that it is almost impossible to buy a really awful bottle of wine in France – perhaps the lowest quality wines are exported? I know that I have never had a bottle that was less than enjoyable when on French soil!

There are two distinct styles of wine produced; the vin ordinaire for everyday drinking, and the more specialised wines from the great chateaux which usually benefit from cellerage and maturation.

Country Wines & the Great Chateaux

Much of the *vin ordinaire* is produced in the south of France and there has been a great effort recently to re-name it *vin du pays* (country wine) – this sounds more classy and somehow instantly makes the wine a little more expensive! These wines are generally best drunk as young as possible and benefit from being consumed with food – they are characterful but often not particularly rounded so local dishes from the southern regions of France, flavoured with garlic, tomatoes, olives and other Mediterranean ingredients do complement the wines particularly well.

To adequately describe the great chateaux and fine wines of France would require a whole bookful of space! Many fine wines have been auctioned for vast amounts of money – a 1794 bottle of Chateau d'Yquem was sold at Christies for £36,000 in 1986, a positive bargain compared to a 1787 Château Lafite sold for £105,000 in the same year! Imagine opening it to find that it had gone off! I can't see the point in spending that sort of money on wine – I should also mention that I can't begin to contemplate having that sort of money to spend on wine! Suffice it to say that, whatever your taste and whatever your budget, the French have such an enormous and diverse wine industry that there will always be an excellent selection of wines to choose from, quite literally something to suit everyone.

The New World Challenge

Wine industries are now flourishing in many new world countries such as America, Australia and Chile, to name but a few. All are producing excellent wines but I do find that they tend to be very similar, often using the same type of grapes. Of course, that is a sweeping statement but chardonnays and cabernet sauvignons do seem to crop up with amazing regularity. Within France there is such a variety of wine styles to choose from.

Investment in the New World has produced consistent quality at reasonable prices. Much of the wine comes from hi-tech wineries with vast gleaming stainless steel vats which seem centuries away from the oak barrels in romantic chateau cellars that are still common in France. However, the very strong challenge from the New World has been good for us, the consumers, by forcing the French to up-date their image and pay greater attention to quality in all areas of their wine production. Care has always been lavished on the wines of the great chateaux but the cost of such wines is prohibitive for the average enthusiast. The move to Vin du Pays has encouraged much better wines within even the lowest price range.

Two Great Names in French Cuisine

I really believe that the French are the best advertisement possible for their cuisine as they are so universally enthusiastic about eating and drinking! However, there are two names which really stand out in the history of French food, one a gastronome and one a chef.

Brillat-Savarin, the Gastronome

Jean Antrhelme Brillat-Savarin was born in 1755 and died in Paris in 1826. Throughout his life he was an enthusiastic amateur in the world of food – his employment was as a magistrate and politician. His greatest work – *The Psychology of Taste* – was published a year before his death in 1825 and is a treatise on the art of cookery, combining observations, anecdotes and his sheer pleasure in eating. Many dishes were named after Brillat-Savarin, in recognition of all he did for the French cuisine.

Auguste Escoffier, a Brilliant Chef

Escoffier was born in France in 1846 but it was abroad, in England, that he established himself as one of the greatest chefs of all time. He began cooking at twelve and moved to London after six years in Paris and some time at the Grand Hotel in Monte Carlo.

Escoffier was the first chef at the Savoy Hotel, where he presided over the kitchens for eight years before moving on to the Carlton House Hotel, then one of the leading hotels in London. He spent sometime abroad in Europe and America, collecting ideas for the 10,000 recipes with which he is credited. Escoffier certainly perfected many of the great sauces and culinary decorations still in use today. He was made a Chevalier of the Legion d'Honneure in 1920, and an Officer of the Legion in 1928.

Escoffier retired in 1921 at the age of 75, and then spent much of his time writing. He died, leaving an enormous legacy of creative genius, in 1935.

Bon Appetit!

Well, I've set the scene for a culinary tour of discovery, exploring just some of the classic dishes of France, the gastronomic capital of the world. I apologise if any of your favourites are not here but I have tried to make a selection that covers the whole range of classic French cookery. Some standard recipes that are essential to many everyday dishes are included in a chapter of Basic Recipes at the back of the book.

There are two ingredients that I hope I have passed on to you and that are essential for creative French cookery; passion and enthusiasm. Bon appetit!

Soups, Starters & Appetisers

It is hard enough to know how to combine recipes into chapters for any cookbook, but when the book is about Classic French cookery, the most revered cuisine in the world, it is doubly difficult! "Soups, Starters & Appetisers" sounds like an enormous chunk of recipes, but those contained within this chapter are suitable for serving as the first course of a meal or as cocktail savouries.

I have also included recipes for Anchoyade, Tapenade and Aïoli. These are pastes or dressings and may be spread on toasts or croûtons or added as an extra flavouring at the end of cooking – I love to stir a spoonful of tapenade into a daube just before serving. Pungent, savoury and delicious – experiment with these foods if you have not yet discovered their delights! I quite often serve a selection of such sauces with a roasted pepper salad and olive oil bread as a dinner party starter.

Tasty – But Not Too Filling

Starters can be stunning either in their simplicity or in their elaborate and time-consuming preparation. The main thing is not to prepare anything which is too filling – the main course should be the focus of the meal. That said, many people find the starter to be the most enjoyable and memorable course, perhaps because it is the first food enjoyed on an empty stomach, or maybe because it makes the most impact on a freshly laid table.

Exotic Ingredients as Affordable Treats

Many of the more expensive ingredients, such as scallops, lobsters and asparagus, make excellent starters and can be enjoyed as such because they are affordable in small quantities! Shellfish are found in abundance around the coasts of Normandy and Brittany, both areas also rich in dairy produce which explains the classic serving of many of these foods in rich creamy sauces. When serving such luxurious foods hot, as a starter or as a main course, take great care not to overcook the shellfish. Purchased very fresh and in prime condition, shellfish requires very little cooking – overcooking will toughen and spoil these delectable foods.

I have included a number of salads which make perfect starters. One or two of these, such as Chicken Liver Salad are served with the main ingredient freshly cooked and added to the salad whilst hot. Such salads have become very fashionable in recent years, although they have been popular for a long time in France. I think they make an ideal starter, having always subscribed to the theory that a hot or warm starter immediately indicates that you have gone to considerable effort in the time-consuming preparation of the meal that follows. Of course, this need not be so and a warm salad provides a delicious and effective illusion!

Soups as Starters

Soups, once the main course or, indeed, the only course in the average family meal, are now starters, a celebration of fresh vegetables in season and a warming dish to serve before a main course of cold meats or fish. Canned soups may be a reliable stand-by for the typical summer's day away from the south of France, when high temperatures and brilliant sunshine are not always as reliable as they might be, but soup should not only be thought of as emergency heating! I find that the best soups are made from vegetables and other ingredients when they are in season and full of flavour. Lobster Bisque and Crab Soup are both delicious treats but perfectly affordable to make when there is a glut of shellfish.

Soup Kitchens and Restaurants

It should be remembered that soups actually gave rise to the modern restaurant as the centre of good food. The very first eating establishment to be known as a restaurant was founded in Paris in 1765 by a French soup maker, who sold a selection of soups or restoratives from his up-market soup kitchen. This became known as a restaurant, because of the restorative nature of his dishes. So much in the world of food has its origins in France! The French are still great soup eaters, and many country folk do not consider that they have had a meal, even in the summer, if it has not been preceded by a plate of soup. Perhaps the habit of serving soup in proper soup plates, rather than in an all-purpose bowl, indicates the importance of soup in France?

When planning the first course of your meal the most important thing to consider is the provision of a contrast to the course that follows, both in flavour and texture. Having satisfied that criteria, indulge yourself!

FRENCH ONION SOUP

I have read more than once that this soup was traditionally consumed in the small hours, after a heavy night on the town! Whether or not that is true, it is certainly one of the best known classic soups of France. The secret of a good onion soup is to get as much colour as possible from the onions by browning them well.

Serves 6

Ingredients
120g/4oz butter
6 large onions, thinly sliced
2 cloves garlic, crushed
Salt and freshly ground black pepper
6 tbsps red wine
1.14 litres/2 pints well-flavoured stock
6 slices French bread, toasted
120g/4oz Gruyère cheese, finely grated

Melt the butter in a large pan, add the onion and garlic and cook gently for about 30 minutes, stirring from time to time to prevent them from sticking to the pan. Season with salt and pepper. Add the wine and boil until slightly reduced. Add the stock and bring the soup to the boil, stirring continuously. Reduce the heat and simmer for 30 minutes. If the soup becomes too thick, stir in a little extra stock or water.

Serve the soup in individual bowls. Float a slice of toast in each bowl and scatter with the grated cheese. Place under a hot grill for a few minutes to melt and brown the cheese.

PEASANT'S SOUP

Cabbages are widely used in France so it is no surprise to find this vegetable in a soup! Such country fare derives its richness from a little bacon and some dripping from either a goose or a duck. Once a standard in almost every larder, these ingredients are now luxuries and, if not available, should be replaced with two or three tablespoons of well-flavoured olive oil.

Serves 6

Ingredients

120g/4oz cabbage, shredded
2 tbsps goose or other poultry dripping
120g/4oz smoked bacon, chopped
175g/6oz leeks, chopped
1 turnip, peeled and diced
1.14 litres/2 pints chicken stock
225g/8oz potatoes, peeled and diced
6 slices of bread
Salt and freshly ground black pepper

Blanch the cabbage in a large pan of boiling water for 3 minutes. Drain and set the cabbage aside, discarding the water. Melt the dripping in the pan, add the bacon and cook gently – do not allow the bacon to brown. Stir in all the vegetables except the cabbage and potatoes and cook gently for a few minutes. Add the blanched cabbage to the pan then pour in the stock. Bring to the boil, cover the soup and simmer very gently for about 90 minutes – the long, slow cooking time will really allow the flavours of the vegetables to blend together and develop. Add the potatoes for the last 20 minutes of the cooking time. If the stock reduces too much during cooking, add a little extra water.

Place a slice of fresh bread in the bottom of each individual soup bowl. Season the soup to taste with salt and freshly ground black pepper and ladle the soup into the bowls, over the bread. Serve immediately.

LEEK AND POTATO SOUP

This popular soup combines two favourite ingredients. In the winter it is a warming, comforting dish. In the summer, when made with young, tender vegetables, it can be puréed, chilled and then, with the addition of cream, it becomes the classic Vichyssoise.

Serves 4-6

INGREDIENTS
30g/1oz butter
4 large leeks, thinly sliced
4 large potatoes, peeled and diced
1.14 litres/2 pints chicken stock
570ml/1 pint water
Salt and freshly ground black pepper
4 tbsps double cream

To Serve
30g/1oz butter, softened
4 tbsps single cream
1 tbsp freshly chopped parsley
1 tbsp freshly chopped chives

Melt the butter in a large pan, add the prepared leeks and cook them gently until softened but not browned. Add the potatoes, stock, water, salt and pepper, and bring to the boil. Cover the pan and simmer for approximately 35 minutes, until all the vegetables are cooked.

Stir the double cream into the soup and season it to taste. Serve the soup as it is, or blend until smooth in a liquidiser or food processor. Serve dotted with the remaining butter, and with the single cream swirled into the soup. Sprinkle with the freshly chopped herbs at the last minute.

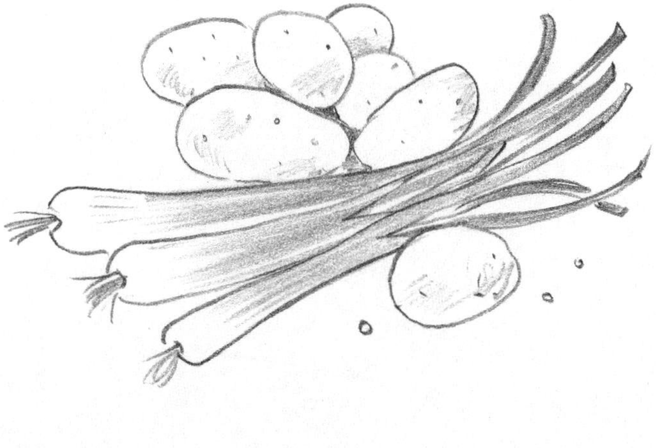

PISTOU SOUP

Pistou is a delicious sauce of fresh basil and garlic. It differs from its Italian cousin pesto in as much as it often contains tomato but no pine nuts. The soup should be served piping hot with the sauce in a separate small bowl. Each person then stirs a spoonful of sauce into their soup before eating.

Serves 8

Ingredients

225g/8oz butter beans, or small white beans, soaked overnight and drained
2 carrots, diced
2 courgettes, trimmed and diced
1 stick of celery, trimmed and sliced
460g/1lb French beans
2 leeks, white parts only, finely sliced
1 large onion, finely sliced
1 large potato, sliced
2.3 litres/4 pints chicken stock
1 bouquet garni
Salt and freshly ground black pepper

Pistou

6 cloves garlic
20-30 fresh basil leaves, depending on size
3 tomatoes, skinned, seeded and chopped
90g/3oz Parmesan cheese, freshly grated
120ml/4fl oz olive oil

Rinse the soaked beans and cook them in a large pan of fresh water for 30 minutes, until just beginning to soften. Drain the beans and then return them to the pan. Add the carrots, courgettes, celery, French beans, leeks, onion and potato, then the stock, bouquet garni and salt and pepper. Bring to the soup to the boil, reduce the heat and cover the pan then simmer for 30 – 40 minutes, until the vegetables and the beans are cooked through and softened.

Make the Pistou while the soup is cooking. Pound the garlic, basil leaves and tomatoes together in a pestle and mortar. Stir in the cheese and slowly add the olive oil, a little at a time, beating continuously until the mixture is smooth. The sauce can also be made in a liquidiser or food processor, if preferred. Season with salt and pepper.

Season the soup and serve with the pistou.

CREAM OF CAULIFLOWER AND PARSLEY SOUP

Madame du Barry, a contemporary of Louis XV, had a classic creamy cauliflower soup named after her. This soup is a variation on that classic dish, adding a generous flavouring of parsley. Use the French flat-leaf parsley if you can – it is easy to grow and is also available in many large supermarkets in the fresh herbs section. You may prefer to use white pepper for this soup as it is more deliciate in flavour than black.

Serves 6

Ingredients
60g/2oz butter
225g/8oz leeks, white parts only, cut into thin slices
1.14 litres/2 pints chicken stock
460g/1lb cauliflower florets, washed and chopped
A generous bunch, about 5 tbsps, flat-leaved parsley
200ml/7 fl oz double cream
Salt and pepper

Melt half of the butter in a large pan and cook the leeks until softened but not browned. Add the stock and the cauliflower, stir well and bring to the boil. Reduce the heat and simmer the soup gently for about 30 minutes, until the cauliflower is just cooked. Reserve 150ml/¼ pint of the soup and blend the remainder in a liquidiser or food processor until smooth. Rinse the pan and return the soup to it.

Blanch the parsley in boiling, salted water for 1 minute, then drain well. Mix the parsley with the reserved cauliflower soup and blend in a liquidiser or food processor until smooth. Reheat the soup if necessary and stir in the cream and the remaining butter, in small pieces, then season well. Serve the cauliflower soup in individual bowls, swirling a spoonful of the blended parsley into each.

SOUPE DE POISSONS PROVENÇALE

France is famed for its fish soups which vary from smooth, creamy broths to robust mixed fish soups, some of which are almost a stew and a meal in themselves! This soup has the rich flavours of Provençe and is accompanied by rouille, a rich hot sauce of red peppers and olive oil.

Serves 4

INGREDIENTS

Soup

1 large onion, chopped
2 leeks, chopped
150ml/¼ pint olive oil
2 cloves garlic, crushed
2 × 400g/14oz cans chopped tomatoes
1.4kg/3lbs mixed white fish
225g/8oz prawns or scampi
1 bay leaf
1 sprig thyme
1 small piece of fennel or 2 stalks of parsley
1 strip orange rind
1.7 litres/3 pints water
150ml/¼ pint dry white wine
2 pinches saffron strands
Salt and freshly ground black pepper
Tomato purée
30g/1oz flour
30g/1oz butter
Single cream

Sauce Rouille

1 small red chilli
60g/2oz red pepper or canned pimento, chopped
3-4 tbsps fresh white breadcrumbs
3 cloves garlic, crushed
1 egg yolk
Salt and freshly ground black pepper
150ml/¼ pint extra virgin olive oil

To Serve

Grated Parmesan cheese
Croûtons

Prepare the soup. Cook the chopped onion and leeks in the olive oil until softened but not browned. Add the garlic with the tomatoes, then bring the mixture to the boil. Cook gently for 5 minutes whilst preparing the fish. Fillet and skin the fish, cutting it into large pieces. Shell the prawns or scampi, and tie the bay leaf, thyme, fennel and orange peel together with a piece of string. Add the prepared fish and aromatics to the tomato mixture with the water, wine, saffron and salt and pepper. Simmer, uncovered, for 30-40 minutes.

Prepare the Sauce Rouille. Seed the chilli and chop it finely – only use half if you prefer a milder flavour. Chop the red pepper or pimento. Soak the breadcrumbs in a little water, then squeeze them dry and place them in a liquidiser or food processor with the chilli, pepper, garlic and egg yolk. Season with salt and pepper and then blend to a smooth paste. This mixture may also be worked together with a pestle and mortar. Gradually add the olive oil in a thin, steady stream until the sauce has the consistency of mayonnaise.

Remove the bundle of herbs from the pan of soup, then blend the soup until smooth in a liquidiser or food processor. Strain the soup if necessary, then season and add a little tomato purée for colour. Rinse the pan, return the soup to it and bring it to the boil. Mix the flour and butter together and add to the soup a little at a time, whisking and boiling the soup between each inclusion. The soup should have the consistency of thick cream. Stir a little single cream into the soup just before serving.

Spoon a little of the Sauce Rouille into each individual bowl of soup, and serve garnished with Parmesan and croutons.

PUMPKIN SOUP

Pumpkins are really only just becoming popular again in England having slipped out of fashion, although they have always been in demand in America and France. They mature in the autumn, making this soup ideal for serving before a main course of the new season's game. Drain the pumpkin well, otherwise the soup will be watery.

Serves 6

INGREDIENTS

1.4kg/3lbs pumpkin, peeled and cut into cubes
280ml/½ pint milk
280ml/½ pint double cream
1 tsp ground cinnamon
Salt and freshly ground black pepper

Cook the pumpkin in boiling salted water until tender; this will take about 20 minutes. Drain the pumpkin well and mash it with a fork until smooth. Place the pumpkin in a liquidiser or a food processor with the milk and blend until smooth.

Rinse the pan and return the soup to it. Stir in the cream and cinnamon, and reheat the soup until almost boiling. Season well and serve hot.

CHICKEN BREAST SALAD

For the best and most eye-catching presentation of this salad use corn-fed chicken breasts – the meat is a most wonderful golden yellow colour and looks stunning when combined with the avocado, lettuce and tomato. Many chickens are fed on corn in France to improve the flavour of the meat. This starter is quite filling so serve it before a light main course, or as a light supper dish.

Serves 6

INGREDIENTS
Knob of butter
3 corn-fed chicken breasts
150ml/¼ pint dry white wine
175ml/6fl oz chicken stock
90ml/3fl oz double cream
Salt and freshly ground black pepper
4 tomatoes
2 avocados, peeled, stoned and sliced
Juice of 1 lemon
Mixed salad leaves for serving

Melt the butter in a frying pan and quickly seal the chicken on all sides. Add the white wine to the frying pan and cook quickly until reduced by half. Pour in the stock and cook over a moderate heat until reduced by half. Reduce the heat to as low as possible, cover the pan and cook for a further 10-12 minutes, or until the chicken is cooked through. Remove the chicken breasts, return the pan to the heat and stir in the cream, seasoning with salt and pepper. Bring to the boil, stirring continuously, and continue to boil until the sauce has thickened.

Skin and seed two of the tomatoes, then cut them into thin sticks and dice them. Cut the remaining tomatoes into thin slices.

Alternate slices of tomato and avocado, tossed in the lemon juice, around a bed of prepared salad leaves on a serving plate. Slice the warm chicken breasts and arrange them in the middle. Scatter with the diced tomato and then pour the sauce over the salad.

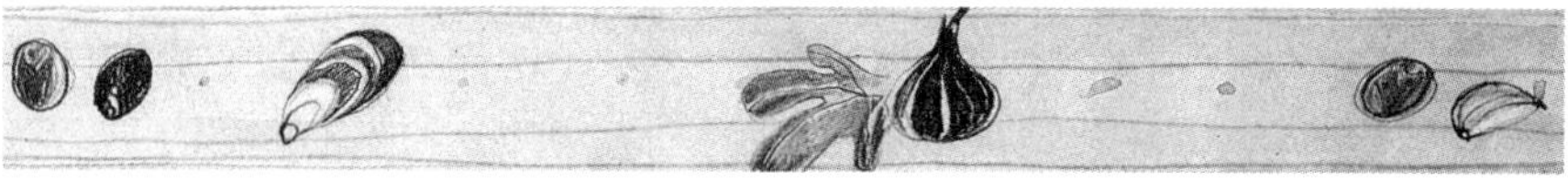

FISHERMAN'S SALAD

A new dish, an elegant starter to any meal. Care must be taken in the preparation of the vegetables, but the stunning result makes it well worth the effort.

Serves 6

INGREDIENTS

1 carrot, scraped
½ cucumber, wiped, peeled and seeded
1 red pepper, seeded
1 courgette, wiped
40 small prawns, peeled (retain the peelings)
1 tbsp olive oil
1 tbsp brandy or cognac
175ml/6fl oz single cream
Juice of ½ a lemon
2 tbsps freshly chopped chervil

Cut each of the vegetables carefully into very fine julienne strips. As you finish each vegetable, put the strips in the fridge to keep them crisp and fresh. Fry the prawn peelings briskly over a high heat for 5 minutes in the olive oil. Add the brandy or cognac and flambé the mixture. Allow the alcohol to burn out, then stir in the cream, and continue cooking over a low heat for about 10 minutes.

Strain the sauce through a fine sieve, discarding all but the smooth sauce. Blend the sauce with a hand mixer and then put the sauce in the fridge to cool.

On a serving dish, spread a single bed of the vegetable strips and sprinkle over the peeled prawns. Add the lemon juice to the cooled sauce, stir well and pour it over the salad. Sprinkle over the chervil and serve.

CHICKEN LIVER SALAD

I have always associated chicken livers with France and French cookery, possibly because my first introduction to them was in a Pâté Maison, a smooth chicken liver pâté flavoured with brandy and set with lots of creamy butter. This salad includes warm pan-fried livers and a warm dressing, added to the salad at the last moment – very chic!

Serves 4-6

INGREDIENTS
2 large globe artichokes
Juice of 1 lemon
Knob of butter
150ml/¼ pint olive oil
340g/12oz chicken livers
1 small onion, finely chopped
Mixed salad leaves
4 tbsps red wine vinegar
Salt and freshly ground black pepper

Prepare the artichokes by removing the stalks and then cutting off all the outer leaves with a small, sharp knife. Cook the artichokes with the lemon juice in boiling salted water until tender, about 15-20 minutes. Remove and discard the hairy chokes and slice the remaining artichoke hearts.

Melt the butter in a frying pan, add 2 tbsps of the olive oil and cook the livers and onion over a moderately high heat for about 5 minutes. Arrange the prepared salad leaves on individual plates while the livers are cooking. Deglaze the frying pan with 1 tbsp of the vinegar, stirring it into the pan over a high heat and scraping up any pieces of livers from the bottom of the pan. Cook for a further 1-2 minutes, then arrange the livers on the salad leaves and top them with slices of the artichoke.

Warm the remaining vinegar in the frying pan and add the remaining oil. Season and whisk the dressing together until well blended. Pour a little of the warm dressing over each individual salad.

SMOKED HERRING SALAD

A nouvelle cuisine recipe especially developed for the sophisticated dinner party. Smoked salmon could be used in place of the smoked herring, if preferred.

Serves 6

INGREDIENTS
3 heads chicory, wiped
4 smoked herring, filleted
4 large new potatoes, cooked
1 onion, finely chopped
8 coriander seeds
1 tsp sea salt
150ml/¼ pint olive or corn oil
1 tsp mustard
1 tbsp wine vinegar
Pepper

Separate the chicory leaves and slice them lengthways into thin strips. Slice the herring fillets crosswise and mix with the chicory leaves. Dice the potatoes, mix with the above and add the onion, coriander seeds and salt.

In a salad bowl, mix together the oil, mustard, vinegar and pepper. Add all the other ingredients and mix well to incorporate the sauce, or arrange on serving plates and drizzle over the dressing.

LAMBS' SWEETBREAD SALAD

You will have to find a friendly traditional butcher in order to obtain the sweetbreads for this recipe.

Serves 4

INGREDIENTS
340g/12oz lambs' sweetbreads
Salt and freshly ground black pepper
1 tbsp plain flour
1 tsp sherry vinegar, or good quality red wine vinegar
2 tbsps mayonnaise
1 tbsp chicken stock
1 tsp freshly chopped chervil
1 crisp lettuce, broken into bite sized pieces
30g/1oz butter

Blanch the sweetbreads in boiling water for 1 minute, then drain and remove and discard the nerves. Chop the sweetbreads into bite-sized pieces, season with salt and pepper and coat in the flour.

Stir the vinegar into the mayonnaise, then stir in the stock – this should give a slightly thickened sauce. Stir in the chervil and season with salt and pepper. Arrange the lettuce on individual serving plates.

Sauté the sweetbreads in the butter for 2-3 minutes, or until golden, then drain and arrange them on the prepared lettuce. Pour the chervil sauce over the sweetbreads and serve immediately.

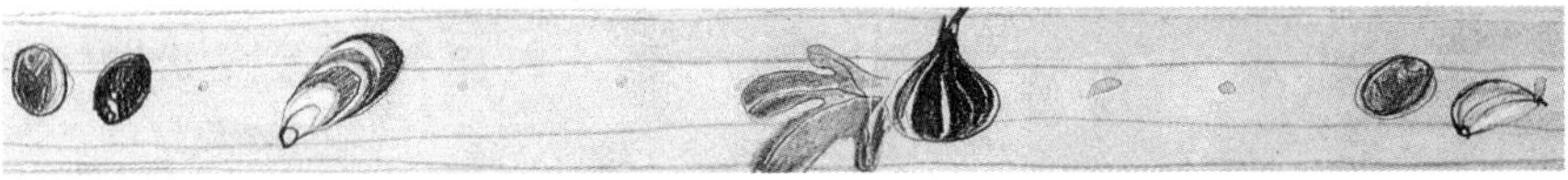

CHICKEN & WALNUT SALAD

A light and elegant salad – use whatever cheese you prefer, according to the flavours of the rest of the meal. I usually choose a ripe Brie, a Bleu d'Auvergne or a Pont l'Evêque but you can choose any cheese that you like. Replace the chicken with shellfish and you almost have the classic Salade Normande.

Serves 6

INGREDIENTS
1 green apple, diced
1 red apple, diced
Juice of 1 lemon
460g/1lb cooked chicken breasts
120g/4oz shelled walnuts
175g/6oz cheese, diced or crumbled
Mixed salad leaves

Dressing
120ml/4fl oz natural yogurt
1 tbsp Dijon mustard
120ml/4fl oz olive oil
2 tbsps white wine vinegar
2 tbsps ground walnuts
Salt and freshly ground black pepper

Dice the apples and toss them in the lemon juice to prevent them from discolouring. Cut the chicken breasts into neat cubes and mix with the apple and shelled walnuts, then carefully mix in the cheese.

Mix the ingredients for the dressing together in a bowl or shake well in a screw-topped jar. Season the dressing to taste and pour it over the chicken and apple mixture.

Place a little salad on 6 small serving plates, top with the chicken and serve immediately with fresh, crusty French bread.

HERBY GOAT'S CHEESE

Goats' cheese is very popular in France and many small farmers make their own cheeses to sell in the local markets. This recipe uses small soft cheeses – a soft cheese from a tub would be more appropriate than a mould-ripened cheese.

Serves 4

INGREDIENTS
- 2 fresh goat cheeses, weighing about 225g/8oz in total
- 1 tbsp finely chopped onion
- 1 tbsp finely chopped shallot
- 1 tbsp freshly chopped mixed herbs, such as chives, parsley and chervil
- 10 capers
- 5 peppercorns
- Salt and freshly ground black pepper
- Few drops vinegar
- A squeeze of lemon juice
- ½ tsp olive oil

Mix the cheeses with the onion, shallot and freshly chopped herbs, then mix in the capers, peppercorns and the salt and pepper. Stir in the vinegar, lemon juice and olive oil and mix well.

Divide the cheese between 4 small ramekins, pushing it down well, and then chill in the refrigerator for about 2 hours. Turn out just before serving onto a bed of fresh salad leaves.

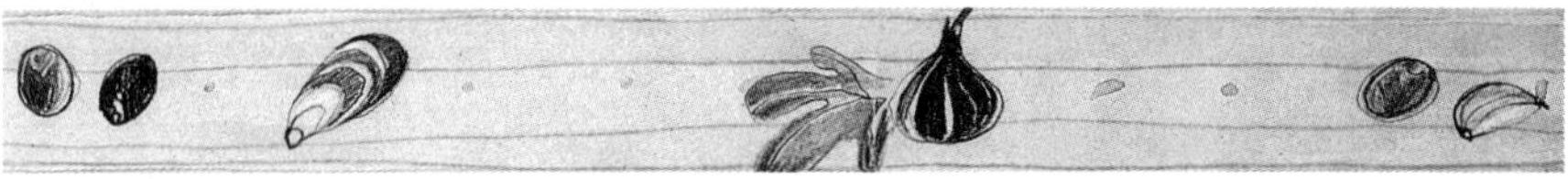

HADDOCK MOUSSE

A deliciously light fish mousse in the new style of French cookery. This recipe may not be an established classic, but it soon will be! Serve the haddock mousse with a light dressing of olive oil, lemon juice, salt and pepper. Leaf gelatine dissolves more readily than the powdered variety – seek it out if you possibly can.

Serves 4

INGREDIENTS
3 leaves gelatine
3 small fillets of smoked haddock
275ml/½ pint fish stock
200ml/7fl oz double cream
1 tbsp freshly chopped chives
Salt and freshly ground black pepper

Soak the gelatine in a bowl of cold water. Cut one of the haddock fillets in half and chop it finely. Use either a very sharp knife or a food processor.

In a saucepan, gently heat the fish stock and the chopped haddock fillet. Drain the gelatine sheets and stir into the stock until they have completely dissolved. Remove from the heat, transfer to a clean bowl and put in the refrigerator.

Meanwhile, whip the cream until it becomes light and fluffy. Keep cool. Once the stock is completely cool, gently fold in the whipped cream, chives and salt and pepper. Return the mixture to the refrigerator for at least 2 hours.

Cut the remaining fillets into very thin slices, like smoked salmon, and spread them out slightly overlapping in 4 even-sized rectangles onto pieces of cling film. Place spoonfuls of mousse across the centre of each. There should be some mousse left over. Using the cling film to help you, gently roll up the slices of haddock to make neat rolls. Put the rolls back into the refrigerator until ready to serve.

Using a teaspoon, form the remaining mousse into small oblong shapes, and serve with the haddock roll. Remove the cling film before serving.

PÂTÉ DE CAMPAGNE

A rough country-style pâté, there must be literally thousands of variations on this recipe. The local wine or brandy, the herbs and the seasonings all add their own particular touch. Pâté de campagne, country pâté, is made throughout France. Serve with hot toast and a salad garnish.

Serves 10

INGREDIENTS

340g/¾lb pig's liver, skinned and tubes removed
340g/¾lb pork, coarsely minced
120g/4oz veal, coarsely minced
225g/8oz pork fat, coarsely minced
2 shallots, finely chopped
1 clove garlic, crushed
3 tbsps Cognac
½ tsp ground allspice
Salt and freshly ground black pepper
1 tsp freshly chopped thyme or sage
225g/8oz streaky bacon, rind and bones removed
2 tbsps double cream
120g/4oz smoked ham, cut into 6mm/¼ inch cubes
1 large bay leaf

Preheat the oven to 180°C/350°F/Gas Mark 4. Place the liver in a food processor and process once or twice to chop it roughly. Add the minced meats and fat, shallots, garlic, Cognac, allspice, salt and pepper and thyme and process once or twice to mix. Do not over-work the mixture; it should be coarse. You could chop the liver by hand and mix the pâté in a bowl, if preferred.

Stretch the strips of bacon with the back of a knife and use to line a terrine, metal loaf tin or ovenproof glass dish. Stir the cream and the diced ham into the meat mixture by hand, then press it into the prepared dish on top of the bacon. Place the bay leaf on top of the pâté and fold over any overlapping edges of bacon.

Cover the dish with a tight-fitting lid or two layers of foil and place the dish in a bain marie (a roasting tin of hand hot water); the water should come halfway up the sides of the terrine. Bake for 2 hours, or until the meat juices run clear.

Take the pâté from the oven and remove the lid or foil. Cover with fresh foil and press the pâté with heavy cans or balance scale weights. Allow to cool at room temperature and then refrigerate, still weighted, until completely chilled and firm.

To serve, remove the weights and foil. Turn the pâté out onto a serving plate and scrape off any excess fat. Slice and serve.

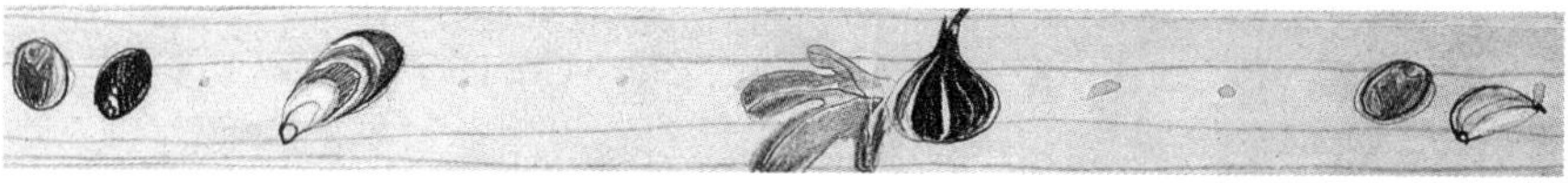

CHICKEN LIVER PÂTÉ WITH CORIANDER

A variation on Pâté Maison, a popular chicken liver pâté made throughout France. Most people have their own way of seasoning the pâté – coriander is a most unusual and delicious flavouring. Serve with freshly cooked toast, or fresh crusty bread and a glass of the local wine.

Serves 4

INGREDIENTS
460g/1lb chicken livers, trimmed
225g/8oz butter, softened
4 shallots, finely chopped
2 plump cloves garlic, chopped
2 tsps ground coriander
2 tsps freshly chopped parsley
Salt and freshly ground black pepper
2 tsps mango chutney
Coriander leaves and clarified butter to garnish

If the livers are large cut them into evenly-sized pieces. Melt half the butter in a sauté pan and add the shallots, garlic, ground coriander and livers, and cook together over a moderate heat for about 5 minutes, until the livers are cooked through. Allow to cool completely then blend in a liquidiser or food processor until smooth. Push the mixture through a metal sieve if a totally smooth pâté is required. Add the remaining butter, parsley, salt and pepper and chutney. Process again until smooth, and transfer to a serving dish. Coat with clarified butter and decorate with coriander leaves when the butter has set. Chill for 2 hours, then serve with toast.

SPINACH & CHICKEN TERRINE

A lightly baked terrine, a variation on the classic Pâté de Campagne but made with chicken. I like to serve such terrines with a thin home-made mayonnaise, lightly spiced with green peppercorns.

Serves 4-6

INGREDIENTS

225g/8oz chicken breasts, boned and skinned
2 egg whites
120g/4oz fresh white breadcrumbs
Salt and freshly ground black pepper
460g/1lb spinach, washed
3 tbsps freshly chopped chervil, chives and tarragon, mixed
280ml/½ pint double cream
60g/2oz walnuts, finely chopped
Nutmeg
Fromage blanc or low fat cream cheese mixed with milk to a piping consistency

Preheat the oven to 160°C/325°F/Gas mark 3. Blend the chicken, 1 egg white, half the breadcrumbs and salt and pepper in a food processor until well mixed. Cook the spinach in the water that clings to the leaves after washing for 3 minutes or until just wilted. Remove the chicken from the food processor and rinse the processor bowl.

Place the spinach in the processor with the herbs, the remaining egg white and the breadcrumbs, salt, pepper and nutmeg. Process until well mixed. Mix half the cream with the chicken mixture and half with the spinach. Add the walnuts to the spinach with the cream.

Line a 460g/1lb loaf tin with baking parchment and spread the chicken mixture evenly over the base of the tin. Cover with the spinach mixture and carefully smooth the top. Cover with greased foil, sealing tightly. Place the tin in a dish, and add enough warm water to come halfway up the sides of the tin. Bake in the preheated oven for 1 hour or until firm. Allow the terrine to cool, then chill overnight.

Carefully lift the chilled terrine out of the tin using the lining paper. Peel off the paper and place the terrine on a serving plate. Beat the cheese until smooth, adding milk as necessary to give a pipable consistency, and pipe lines or a lattice over the top of the terrine. Serve sliced.

SNAILS WITH POTATOES IN NUTMEG

This is a completely new way of serving snails – a great dish to delight guests at your next dinner party. This dish is ready to serve as soon as the potatoes are cooked.

Serves 4

INGREDIENTS
8 medium-sized potatoes
400ml/scant ¾ pint single cream
Freshly grated nutmeg
Salt and freshly ground black pepper
40 canned snails, cooked and rinsed

Peel the potatoes and cut them into regular-sized slices. Blanch them for 30 seconds in lightly salted boiling water, then drain well. Place the potatoes in a frying pan, add the cream, nutmeg to taste, salt and pepper. Add the snails and cook over a gentle heat until the potatoes are quite tender.

Once the potatoes are cooked, arrange them in a rose pattern with the snails in the middle and the cream sauce poured over.

CREAMED SPINACH

These delicious ramekins of spinach somehow manage a richness of flavour combined with mouth-watering lightness. The French for spinach is l'êpinard – it is a very popular vegetable in France and one which you will often come across on restaurant menus and in the descriptions of the dishes. Always use freshly grated nutmeg with spinach – they were made for each other!

Serves 6

INGREDIENTS

1kg/2¼ lbs spinach, cooked and well drained
5 eggs
225ml/8fl oz double cream
Salt and freshly ground black pepper
Pinch of nutmeg
30g/1oz butter

Preheat the oven to 150°C/300°F/Gas Mark 2. Squeeze out any excess water from the spinach with your fingers, then place the spinach in a mixing bowl. Beat in the eggs, one at a time. Add the cream, salt, pepper and nutmeg and mix well.

Grease 6 ramekin dishes with the butter, and spoon in the spinach mixture. Place the ramekins in a high-sided roasting tin, pour in water to come halfway up the sides of the ramekins and bake them for about 40-50 minutes, until set. Serve hot.

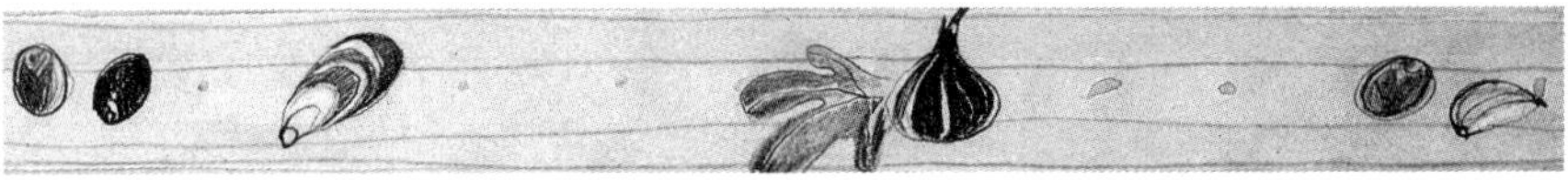

OMELETTE ROUSSILLON

The wine growing area of Roussillon is centred on the town of Perpignan in the south west of France, close to the Spanish border. The Spanish influence is obvious in this tasty omelette, flavoured with peppers and tomatoes. Omelette making is an art – over-cooking will make the eggs rubbery and tough.

Serves 1

Ingredients
3 eggs
Salt and freshly ground black pepper
15g/½ oz butter
¼ green pepper, cut into small dice
60g/2oz ham, cut into small dice
2 tomatoes, skinned, seeded and roughly chopped

Break the eggs into a bowl, season with salt and pepper and beat to mix thoroughly. Heat an omelette pan and drop in the butter, swirling it so that it coats the bottom and sides. When the butter stops foaming, add the pepper and ham and cook for 1-2 minutes, then add the tomatoes.

Pour in the eggs and, as they begin to cook, push the cooked portion with the flat of a fork to allow the uncooked mixture to run underneath, so that it begins to cook. Continue to lift the eggs and shake the pan to prevent the omelette from sticking.

When the egg on top is still slightly creamy, fold one third of the omelette to the centre and tip it out of the pan onto a warmed plate, folded side down. Serve immediately.

EGGS BAKED IN TARRAGON CREAM

There are two types of tarragon, French and Russian, and the French definitely has the finer flavour. It is reminiscent of aniseed, a delicious seasoning for light dishes, especially poultry and eggs. Use freshly laid, free-range eggs for this dish if possible.

Serves 4

Ingredients

1 knob of butter
4 large fresh eggs
1 tbsp freshly chopped French tarragon
Salt and freshly ground black pepper
4 tbsps cream

Preheat the oven to 180°C/350°F/Gas Mark 4. Butter 4 ovenproof ramekins, and break an egg into each one. Stir the chopped tarragon, salt and pepper into the cream and mix well, then spoon 1 tbsp of the cream mixture over each egg.

Place the ramekins on a baking sheet and cook in the preheated oven until set, in about 6-8 minutes. Serve hot.

GOUGÈRE AU JAMBON

A gougère is a large savoury choux pastry, usually served sliced. Such dishes originated in the Burgundy area but regional variations are now popular throughout France. A gougère make an unusual starter or an excellent supper dish.

Serves 4-6

INGREDIENTS

Choux pastry

150ml/¼ pint water
60g/2oz butter or margarine
60g/2oz plain flour, sifted
Salt, freshly ground black pepper and dry mustard
2 eggs, beaten
60g/2oz cheese, finely diced

Ham Salpicon

15g/½ oz butter or margarine
15g/½ oz flour
150ml/¼ pint stock
Salt and freshly ground black pepper
2 tsps freshly chopped herbs
60g/2oz mushrooms, sliced
120g/4oz cooked ham, cut into thin strips
1 tbsp grated cheese
1 tbsp dry breadcrumbs

Preheat the oven to 200°C/400°F/Gas Mark 6. Prepare the pastry. Place the water in a small saucepan then cut the butter into small pieces and add it to the water. Bring slowly to boil, making sure that the butter is completely melted before the water reaches a rapid boil. Increase the heat and allow the mixture to boil rapidly for 30 seconds. Sift the flour with a pinch of salt onto a sheet of paper. Take the pan off the heat and tip all the flour in at once. Stir quickly and vigorously until the mixture comes away from the sides of the pan. Leave to cool slightly.

Melt the butter for the salpicon in a small saucepan and add the flour. Cook for 1-2 minutes until browned to a pale straw colour. Gradually whisk in the stock and add a little salt and pepper and the chopped herbs. Stir in the sliced mushrooms and ham and set aside.

Add a little salt, pepper and the dry mustard to the pastry, then gradually add the beaten eggs, beating well between each addition – this may be done by hand, or with an electric mixer. It may not be necessary to add all the egg – the mixture should be smooth and shiny and hold its shape when ready. Stir in the diced cheese.

Spoon the pastry into a large ovenproof dish or 4 individual dishes, pushing the mixture slightly up the sides of the dish and leaving a well in the centre. The pastry may be piped into a large circle on a lightly greased baking sheet. Fill the centre with the ham salpicon. Mix together the grated cheese and the breadcrumbs and scatter the mixture over the gougère. Bake for about 30 minutes or until the pastry is puffed and browned. Serve immediately.

CHEESE AIGRETTES

These fried choux buns may be served with a salad garnish as a starter, or as a cocktail savoury at a drinks party. They are always popular, so make lots!

Serves 4 as a starter

INGREDIENTS
Cheese Choux Pastry
150ml/¼ pint water
60g/2oz butter, cut into small pieces
75g/2½oz plain flour, sifted
2 eggs, beaten
60g/2oz Gruyère or Cheddar cheese, finely diced or grated
Salt and freshly ground black pepper
Pinch dry mustard
Parmesan cheese (optional)
Oil for deep-frying

Bring the water and the butter slowly to the boil in a heavy-based saucepan – make sure that the butter has melted before the water boils. Heat until boiling rapidly, then draw the pan to one side and shoot in the sifted flour all at once. Beat vigorously until smooth – the mixture will form a ball and leave the sides of the pan. Allow to cool slightly, then beat in the eggs, one at a time, until the pastry is smooth and glossy. Add the cheese and season to taste with salt and pepper and mustard. This pastry can be prepared a few hours in advance and kept in the refrigerator, covered with a damp cloth.

Heat the oil in a deep-fat fryer until moderately hot, about 180°C/350°F. Carefully drop in a teaspoonful of mixture at a time – do not fry too many aigrettes at once as they need space to swell during cooking. Cook the aigrettes for 5-6 minutes, until puffed and golden brown. Remove from the fryer with a slotted spoon and drain on absorbent kitchen paper, then dredge lightly with grated Parmesan cheese. Repeat the frying process until all the mixture has been used. Serve hot.

CROQUE MONSIEUR

This is a simple fried sandwich, an ideal starter or savoury snack. Cut small these make delicious drinks party savouries; left in larger pieces they make an excellent light lunch or supper dish.

Serves 4

INGREDIENTS

8 medium slices white bread
90g/3oz butter
4 slices lean ham
120g/4oz Gruyère cheese, grated
Oil for frying

Butter the bread and lay the ham and cheese on 4 of the slices. Cover with the remaining bread and press the slices firmly together. Cut off the crusts and cut each sandwich into 3 fingers. Fry in hot oil until golden - the sandwiches may be deep or shallow-fried. Drain on absorbent kitchen paper and serve at once.

CHEESE PUFFS

These puffs are similar to the classic Cheese Aigrettes, except they are baked rather than fried. The puffs also have a cheese filling. Serve as a cocktail party savoury.

Makes about 24

INGREDIENTS

Pastry

120g/4oz plain flour
Pinch of salt
90g/3oz butter or margarine, cut into small pieces
225ml/8fl oz water
3 medium eggs, lightly beaten

Filling

75g/2½oz Gruyère cheese, grated
75g/2½oz Emmenthal cheese, grated
1 egg, lightly beaten
2 tsps Kirsch

1 egg yolk, beaten, for glazing

Preheat the oven to 220°C/425°F/Gas Mark 7. Lightly grease two baking sheets.

Sieve together the flour and salt onto a sheet of greaseproof paper. Melt the butter in the water, bringing it slowly to the boil. Remove the pan from the heat once a rolling boil is achieved and shoot in the flour. Beat vigorously until smooth – the mixture will form a ball and come away from the sides of the pan. Allow to cool slightly, then gradually beat in the eggs to give a smooth shiny dough of piping consistency – do not add all the beaten egg if it is not required.

Pipe the pastry into walnut-sized balls on the prepared baking sheets, or use 2 teaspoons to make small mounds of the mixture. Bake in the preheated oven for 10-15 minutes, until firm on the outside. Remove from the oven and reduce the temperature to 200°C/400°F/Gas Mark 6.

To make the filling, beat the grated cheeses together, add the egg and Kirsch. Place the mixture in a piping bag fitted with a 6mm/¼ inch nozzle. Pipe a little of the mixture into each bun, through the base or the side, and brush each one with a little egg yolk.

Return the cheese puffs to the oven for a further 5 minutes. Serve warm, straight from the oven.

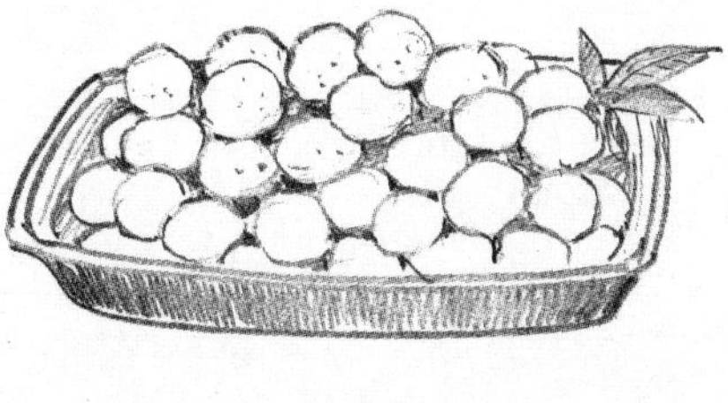

CAMEMBERT FRITTERS

Deep-fried Camembert is one of my favourite starters, although I always have a twinge of guilt when I indulge because of my waistline! This is an interesting variation on the theme. Serve the fritters freshly cooked with a light salad garnish and a little redcurrant or blackberry jelly.

Serves 4-5

INGREDIENTS

Béchamel Sauce

280ml/½ pint milk
1 small onion
1 bay leaf
10 black peppercorns
60g/2oz butter
60g/2oz flour

225g/8oz Camembert
3 egg yolks
1 tsp Dijon mustard
Salt and freshly ground black pepper
Oil for deep-frying
Seasoned flour
2 eggs, beaten
90-120g/3-4 oz fresh white breadcrumbs

Place the milk, onion, bay leaf and peppercorns in a medium-sized saucepan and bring slowly to the boil. Remove the pan from the heat, cover with a lid and leave to infuse for 30 minutes. Strain the milk into a jug.

Melt the butter in a saucepan, add the flour and stir continuously for 1 minute over a low heat. Gradually add the strained milk and heat until the sauce is boiling, thickened and smooth. Cut the rind away from the cheese and discard it, then chop the remaining cheese into small pieces and add it to the béchamel sauce, together with the egg yolks. Simmer gently for 2-3 minutes, stirring constantly, until the cheese has melted. Remove the pan from the heat and add the mustard and seasonings. Pour into a shallow cake tin or Swiss roll tin, to a depth of 1.25cm/½ inch, and allow to cool. The fritter mixture may be made a day in advance and kept in the refrigerator, or frozen until needed.

Using a small pastry cutter about 4cm/1½ inches in diameter, cut out circles of the cheese mixture. Dip the rounds in the seasoned flour, then in the beaten egg and finally coat with the breadcrumbs, pressing them lightly into the surface of the fritters with your fingers.

Heat the oil in a deep-fat fryer or large saucepan with a draining basket to 180°C/350°F and fry the fritters, a few at a time, until golden – this will take 1½-2 minutes. Remove the fritters from the oil with a slotted spoon, drain on absorbent kitchen paper and keep them warm on a serving dish whilst frying the rest of the fritters.

Serve garnished with a little parsley or watercress, and with a cranberry or redcurrant sauce.

TAPENADE

This recipe is popular throughout France but originates in the south, in Provençe, where many of the ingredients are in almost daily use. It may be served as a dip, spread onto bread, or stirred into savoury casseroles or rice dishes at the end of the cooking period. Some people add tuna to their tapenade but this, although delicious, is not traditional.

Serves 4

INGREDIENTS
60g/2oz can anchovy fillets in olive oil
10 black olives, pitted
150ml/¼ pint olive oil
2 tbsps brandy
1 tsp lemon juice
2 tbsps capers
1 tbsp Dijon mustard
1 tsp fresh thyme
Freshly ground black pepper

Blend all the ingredients together in a liquidiser or food processor until smooth, or pound to a smooth paste in a pestle and mortar, gradually adding the olive oil. Season to taste with freshly ground black pepper.

ANCHOYADE

This strongly savoury anchovy paste is heavenly when spread on small crisp toasts and served as a cocktail savoury, garnished with hard boiled egg and mock caviar. It may also be served as a starter with the toasts presented on a bed of lettuce.

Serves 6

Ingredients
15 salted anchovy fillets
2 cloves garlic
120ml/4fl oz olive oil; a fruity, green extra virgin oil is best
Few drops lemon juice
Freshly ground black pepper to taste
12 small slices of bread, toasted

To serve as a starter
1 lettuce, washed and torn into bite-sized pieces
4 tbsps vinaigrette dressing (see recipe)

If serving the anchoyade as a starter, toss the prepared lettuce in the vinaigrette. Rinse the anchovy fillets under cold running water to remove the excess salt, then pat them dry on kitchen paper.

Pound the garlic with a pestle and mortar until it is smooth, then add the anchovies and work them into the garlic. Beat in the oil, a little at a time, until a smooth paste is formed and season to taste with lemon juice and freshly ground black pepper.

Spread the mixture onto the slices of toast. Serve on a bed of the tossed lettuce if wished.

FISH & SHELLFISH

France has three main coasts yielding a fine selection of fish and shellfish. The Mediterranean, the Atlantic Ocean and the English Channel (or should I say, La Manche?) give rise to famous dishes in the north, the south and the west of France. The many rivers throughout the country are home to freshwater fish and the French also add variety by the use of salt cod. It is an understatement to say that the French are fond of fish and a banality to comment that they have some fine recipes for it. In my opinion they are the finest fish cooks in the world and the huge selection of vegetables and other ingredients available to cook with the fish give a versatility of cuisine that is second to none.

Just The Weather for Fishing

One thing that really makes French fish cookery stand out in my mind is that the people understand the effect that the weather can have on the availability of fish. This was illustrated to me when staying with a family in Normandy. Asked what I would like to eat on Sunday I had indicated a preference for seafood and our host had planned to prepare *Fruits de Mer* for us. However, the weather was stormy and had not improved by the Sunday morning. Michel insisted on totally re-planning the lunch menu – if he couldn't obtain fresh fish he certainly was not to be content with frozen. Frozen fish is convenient, but not the same as a really fresh catch. It is rather like herbs – if one fish is not available, use another fresh variety rather than a preserved version of the first choice.

A Celebration of Flavour

Although the French are very much more inventive than, say, the average Englishman in their approach to fish cookery (yes, there is more to it than batter and chips!) it is interesting to note that on the majority of occasions even the greatest of chefs will choose to cook fish simply, barbecuing or grilling it and serving an accompanying sauce, baking it whole or making one of the great fish soups such as *Bouillabaisse*. Perhaps a chef in an expensive city restaurant might consider stuffing a fish with a mousse and serving it in a lobster sauce but the regional chefs and home cooks would celebrate the freshness and flavour of the catch by simple preparation and light but inspired seasoning.

Experiment with Different Fish

Red mullet was a little used fish in England until the 1980s but, as our interest in fish cookery has grown, so has our use of mullet, a fish which has been popular in France for years. Choose larger fish to get as much meat to bone as possible and scale the fish thoroughly before cooking. Red mullet has a very different flavour to white fish and even to some of the oily fish such as mackerel – it actually has a flavour distinctly reminiscent of game! This makes it an excellent fish to barbecue and it is also one of the few fish that can withstand really robust seasoning with olives, strong herbs and garlic. Red Mullet Niçoise, for example, is an unusual and delicious fish recipe that really packs a punch!

I first discovered John Dory (or St Peter's Fish) and monkfish when I was *sous chef d'un jour* for Roger Vergé, Chef Patron of Le Moulin de Mougins near Cannes, when he was undertaking a promotion for Kenwood food mixers. I had never heard of these fish and yet now, almost two decades later, they are enjoying virtually the same popularity in England as they have had in France for many years. I have never been lucky enough to purchase monkfish other than from the tail and this meat is covered with a thick transparent membrane which must be removed before cooking as it will toughen dramatically. The meat itself can be filleted away from the bone and will keep its shape well during cooking.

Whatever your favourite fish the French will have a dish for it, the perfect recipe blending the best ingredients. We should all learn to appreciate fish as much as they do – in that way we would keep many of our traditional recipes alive, certainly those for river fish and the less popular saltwater varieties. It has been a source of both amusement and despair for many years that some of the best fish caught in English waters are shipped to the fish stalls of France where there is a ready and appreciative market for fine fish not in demand in the UK!

COD WITH LEEKS

Large slices of cod are required for this dish. Keep the skin on the fish for an attractive presentation. This dish can be prepared with other types of fish if cod is not available.

Serves 4

Ingredients

- 2 thick pieces of cod, about 340g/¾lb each
- Salt and and freshly ground black pepper
- 900g/2lbs leeks, well rinsed and drained
- 430ml/¾ pint single cream
- 1 tbsp freshly chopped chives

Cut each piece of cod into two, removing any bones. Sprinkle with salt and pepper and keep in a cool place. Cut the leeks into very thin slices, put them in a frying pan and add the cream. Cook over a gentle heat for 10 minutes, covered. Add the fish to the leeks and continue cooking for 10 minutes. Serve the leek and cream base on a preheated plate with the cod fillets placed on top and the chives sprinkled over.

BOW TIE SOLE FILLETS IN OYSTER SAUCE

With the rich flavour of oyster sauce this is an imaginative way of serving sole – an ideal dinner party dish. Use the best quality oysters on the market, they make all the difference to this dish. They should be firm with not too much juice in the shell. The oysters should be cooked for a maximum of 2 minutes, otherwise they will shrink.

Serves 6

INGREDIENTS
3 large sole fillets
225g/8oz mushrooms, rinsed, wiped and finely sliced
2 tomatoes, diced
430ml/¾ pint fish stock
3 tbsps double cream
12 oysters, shells removed
Salt and freshly ground black pepper

Cut the sole fillets lengthways into four strips and tie each piece into a knot; this makes the 'bow tie'. In a large frying pan, cook the mushrooms and half of the tomatoes in the stock for 5 minutes. Gently lower the 'bow ties' into the stock and cook gently for a further 5 minutes or so – cooking time will depend on the thickness of the fillets. Carefully remove the cooked fillets with a slotted spoon.

Remove the sauce from the heat and stir in the cream. Arrange the 'bow ties' neatly on a preheated serving dish. Blend the sauce with a hand mixer until smooth. Stir the oysters into the sauce just prior to serving. Allow just enough time to heat the oysters through and pour the sauce immediately over the 'bow ties'. Sprinkle with the remaining diced tomato and season. Serve immediately.

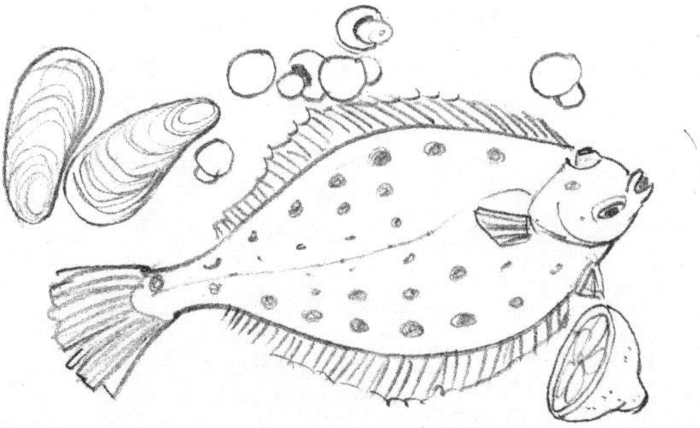

BOUILLABAISSE

Bouillabaisse is the classic fish soup of France, originating from the harbour-side restaurants of Marseille, one of the busiest fishing ports on the Mediterranean coast. Like so many classic dishes, it has been changed and adapted over the years. This recipe makes a delicious fish soup – but purists would say that the only way to eat Bouillabaisse is in a bistro in Marseille!

Serves 4

INGREDIENTS
2kg/4½lbs fresh mixed Mediterranean fish and shellfish, such as whiting, mullet, mussels, prawns, John Dory – fillet the fish and reserve all the bones and trimmings
2 onions, finely chopped
1 sprig fennel
60ml/2fl oz olive oil
2 cloves garlic, crushed
1 tsp freshly chopped thyme
1 bay leaf
Pinch of saffron
Salt and freshly ground black pepper
4 large tomatoes, skinned and sliced
2 large potatoes, diced

Prepare the fish. Skin the fillets and cut the flesh into large pieces. Scrub the mussels and remove any beards. Place the fish bones in a large pan with half the onion and the fennel, cover with plenty of cold water and simmer for 15 minutes to make a fish stock. Strain the stock and discard the bones.

Heat the oil in a large pan, add the remaining onion and the garlic and cook until soft. Add all the seasonings, the tomatoes and the potatoes, then add the stock. Bring to the boil and simmer for 20 minutes, or until the potato is cooked. Add the prepared fish and shellfish and cook for a further 10 minutes. Add extra stock or water to the pan if necessary.

Season the Bouillabaisse to taste. The fish is traditionally served in one bowl with the broth served separately in another. Serve with croûtes of French bread topped with Rouille (see Soup de Poissons Provençale).

MATELOTE

A Matelot is actually a boatman! However, matelote is a name given to a fish stew. There are many recipes for matelote from all over France, each one varying in its use of local fish and wine.

Serves 4

INGREDIENTS

460g/1lb brill or lemon sole
460g/1lb monkfish
1 small wing of skate
225g/8oz unpeeled cooked prawns
1.14 litres/2 pints mussels
3 onions, finely chopped
90g/3oz butter
430ml/¾ pint dry cider or white wine
30g/1oz flour
2 tbsps freshly chopped parsley
Salt and freshly ground black pepper
Lemon juice

Fillet and skin the brill or lemon sole, then cut the fillets into large pieces. Cut the monkfish into similarly sized pieces and cut the skate into four. Peel the prawns, then scrub the mussels, removing any beards and discarding any mussels with cracked or broken shells.

Soften the onions in half the butter, then add the mussels and 3-4 tbsps of water. Cover the pan and shake it over a high heat until all the mussels have opened. Do not overcook the mussels as they will toughen – discard any which remain tightly closed. Strain the cooking liquor into a bowl.

Return the cooking liquor to the pan and add the cider or wine. Add the fish to the pan and simmer gently for 5-8 minutes, until the fish is just cooked. Remove the fish to a serving dish and keep it warm in a low oven. Return the cooking liquor to the boil. Mix the flour with the remaining butter and whisk it, a little at a time, into the liquid. Allow the liquid to boil after each addition.

Add the parsley, prawns, mussels, and lemon juice and seasoning to taste to the sauce and cook briefly to reheat the shellfish. Adjust the seasoning and spoon over the fish in the serving dish. Garnish with a little extra chopped parsley and serve.

TROUT FILLETS WITH FISH ROE SAUCE

The original presentation of the trout fillets provides another visually appealing dish.

Serves 4

INGREDIENTS
4 trout, filleted
Salt and freshly ground black pepper
280ml/½ pint fish stock
150ml/¼ pint double cream
4 tbsps fish roe, lumpfish, keta or salmon trout

Cut the trout fillets in two, crossways. Place four pieces on a sheet of lightly greased foil, overlapping the long sides and alternating, one piece skin side up, the next with flesh side up. Sprinkle with salt and pepper and then close the packet of foil around the fish. Repeat the process with the other pieces of trout to make four parcels all together. Place the stock in a saucepan over a high heat and allow to reduce by half. Stir in the cream and reduce a little more. Purée the sauce in a liquidiser or food processor and keep warm over a saucepan of hot water. Steam the fish in their packets for 10-15 minutes, or until cooked through, then remove the foil. Serve on warmed plates with the sauce poured around the fish and the roe sprinkled over.

SKATE WITH BLACK BUTTER

Skate is one of my favourite fish and this recipe, where it is cooked in black butter, is probably the all-time classic recipe for the fish. The first time that you prepare this you will need a certain amount of courage to actually cook the butter until it browns – don't worry, it will not taste burnt; it will taste wonderful!

Serves 4

INGREDIENTS
4 wings of skate
1 slice onion
2 stalks parsley
Pinch of salt
6 black peppercorns

Black Butter
60g/2oz butter
1 tbsp capers
2 tbsps white wine vinegar
1 tbsp freshly chopped parsley (optional)

Place the skate wings in one layer in a large, deep frying pan. Cover the fish completely with water and add the onion, parsley, salt and peppercorns. Bring slowly to the boil and simmer gently for 10-15 minutes, or until the skate is cooked. Lift the fish out carefully onto a warmed serving dish and remove the skin and any large pieces of bone. Take care not to break up the fish.

Prepare the butter whilst the fish is finishing cooking. Place the butter in a small pan and cook over a high heat until it begins to brown. Add the capers and immediately remove the butter from the heat. Add the vinegar, which will cause the butter to bubble, and add the parsley. Pour the butter immediately over the fish and serve.

RED MULLET PROVENÇALE

Red mullet is a meaty, gamy fish – it is sometimes known as the 'woodcock of the sea' because it is often served with the liver left inside, the traditional way of serving woodcock. In this recipe the mullet is cooked with tomatoes and herbs, some of the traditional ingredients of Provençe.

Serves 4

Ingredients
2 tbsps olive oil
1 clove garlic, crushed
2 shallots, finely chopped
460g/1lb ripe tomatoes, skinned, seeded and sliced
2 tsps freshly chopped marjoram and parsley, mixed
90ml/3fl oz dry white wine
Salt and freshly ground black pepper
Pinch of saffron
Oil for frying
2 small bulbs fennel, quartered and cored
4 red mullet, about 175g/6oz each
Seasoned flour

Heat the olive oil in a deep saucepan and add the garlic and shallots. Cook for 1-2 minutes until slightly softened, then add the tomatoes, herbs, wine, salt and pepper and saffron. Simmer, uncovered, for 30 minutes (adding a little water or stock if necessary), then set to one side while preparing the fennel and fish.

Pour about 4 tbsps oil into a large frying pan or sauté pan. Place over a moderate heat and add the fennel. Cook quickly until the fennel is slightly browned, then lower the heat and cook for a further 5-10 minutes to soften the fennel. Remove it from the pan.

Scale the mullet, remove the gills and clean the fish, leaving the liver. Wash the fish and dry thoroughly. Trim the fins and roll the mullet in seasoned flour, shaking off any excess.

Fry the mullet in the fennel flavoured oil until golden brown, about 5 minutes per side. Arrange the fish in a warm serving dish and surround them with the fennel. Reheat the tomato sauce and spoon some over the fish. Serve any remaining sauce separately.

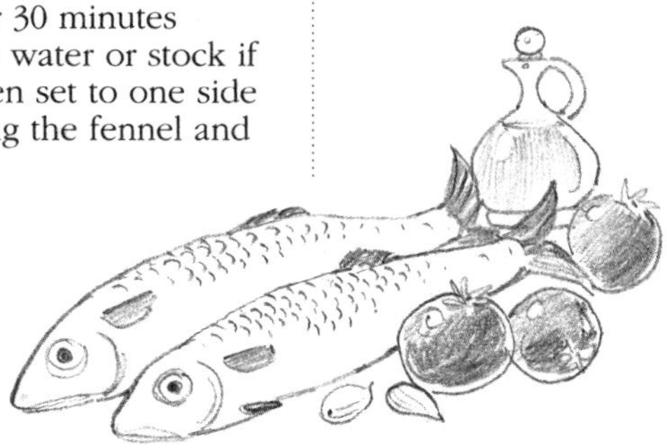

TRUITES MEUNIÈRE AUX HERBES

Meunière is a term often applied to the cooking of fish. Tradition has it that a miller would catch fish from the mill stream and his wife, the meunière, would dredge them in freshly milled flour before cooking. Well, it's a jolly little story – and an excellent way of cooking fish.

Serves 4

INGREDIENTS
4 even-sized trout, cleaned and trimmed
Flour
Salt and freshly ground black pepper
120g/4oz butter
Juice of 1 lemon
2 tbsps freshly chopped herbs such as parsley, chervil, tarragon, thyme or marjoram
Lemon wedges to garnish

Trim the trout tails to make them more pointed, then rinse the fish well. Dredge the trout with flour and shake off any excess, then season with salt and pepper. Heat half the butter in a very large sauté pan and, when foaming, add the trout. It may be necessary to cook the trout in two batches to avoid overcrowding the pan. Cook over a fairly high heat on both sides to brown evenly. Depending on size, the trout should take 5-8 minutes per side to cook. The dorsal fin will pull out easily when the trout are ready. Remove the fish to a serving dish and keep them warm.

Wipe out the pan and add the remaining butter. Cook over a moderate heat until the butter is beginning to brown, then add the lemon juice and herbs. The butter will bubble up and sizzle when the lemon juice is added. Pour the butter over the fish immediately and serve with wedges of lemon.

PROVENÇALE FISH STEW

This is a hearty stew of shellfish, tomatoes, garlic and red wine – a dish for fish lovers everywhere. Choose a fairly robust red wine, a Côtes du Rhône would be my choice. Serve the stew with crusty bread for mopping up the delicious juices.

Serves 4

INGREDIENTS
1 medium onion, finely chopped
2 cloves garlic, crushed
3 tbsps olive oil
680g/1½lbs tomatoes, skinned, seeded and chopped
570ml/1 pint dry red wine
2 tbsps tomato purée
Salt and freshly ground black pepper
1.14 litres/2 pints fresh mussels in their shells, scrubbed and de-bearded
8 large, cooked Mediterranean prawns
120g/4oz cooked, peeled prawns
4 crab claws, shelled but with the claw tips left intact

Fry the onion and garlic together gently in the olive oil until soft but not brown. Add the tomatoes and fry until they are beginning to soften, then stir in the red wine and the tomato purée. Season to taste, bring the mixture to the boil, cover and simmer for about 15 minutes. Add the mussels to the pan, cover and steam for about 5 minutes, shaking the pan frequently, until the mussel shells have opened. Discard any mussels that do not open.

Stir in the remaining ingredients and cook, uncovered, for 3-5 minutes, or until the prawns and crab claws have thoroughly heated through. Season to taste and serve.

RED MULLET NIÇOISE

Red mullet is one of the few fish that is able to cope with strong flavourings, such as olives, peppers, garlic and mustard. This is a well-flavoured, colourful salad, redolent of Mediterranean sunshine!

Serves 4

INGREDIENTS
2 tbsps red wine vinegar
8 tbsps olive oil
4 tsps French mustard
Handful of freshly chopped mixed herbs
1 shallot, finely chopped
1 clove garlic, crushed
Salt and freshly ground black pepper
120g/4oz button mushrooms, quartered
4 red mullet, scaled and cleaned
Seasoned flour
Lemon juice
460g/1lb tomatoes, quartered and cores removed
1 green pepper, seeded and sliced
90g/3oz pitted black olives, halved
2 hard-boiled eggs, quartered
60g/2oz can anchovy fillets

Shake together the vinegar, 4 tbsps of the oil, the mustard, herbs, shallot, garlic and salt and pepper in a screw-topped jar. Place the mushrooms in a bowl and add the vinaigrette. Stir to coat the mushrooms evenly then refrigerate them for about an hour.

Toss the mullet in the seasoned flour. Heat the remaining oil in a frying pan and fry the fish on both sides for about 5 minutes per side, taking care not to break the fish when turning them. Sprinkle lightly with lemon juice and salt and pepper, then leave until cold.

When ready to serve, add the tomatoes, pepper, olives and eggs to the mushrooms. Stir together gently, to coat all the salad ingredients with the marinade. Pile the salad onto a serving dish and arrange the red mullet on top. Garnish with the drained anchovy fillets and serve.

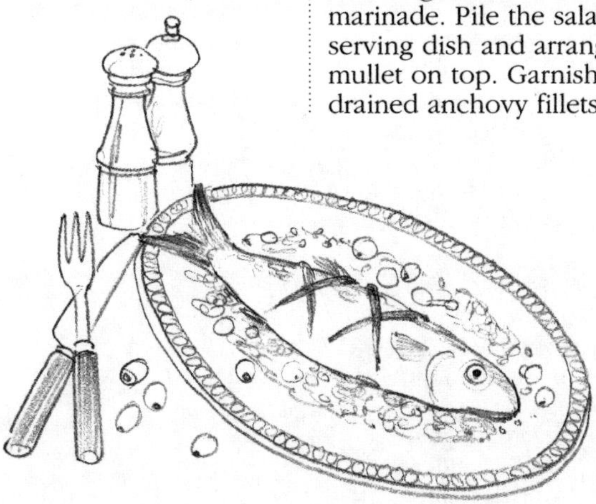

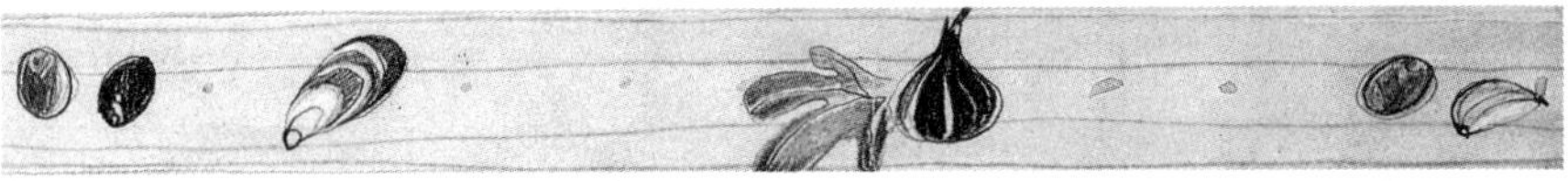

TARRAGON GRILLED RED MULLET

Red Mullet is widely used in France and, because of its attractive appearance, it is now becoming more and more popular in other countries. It has a much stronger flavour than many other fish – here that flavour is balanced by seasoning the fish with tarragon, a strong, slightly aniseed herb.

Serves 4

Ingredients
4 large or 8 small red mullet, gutted, scaled, washed and dried
Salt and freshly ground black pepper
4 or 8 sprigs of fresh tarragon
4 tbsps vegetable oil
2 tbsps tarragon vinegar
1 egg
1 tsp Dijon mustard
120ml/4fl oz sunflower oil
1 tbsp wine vinegar
1 tsp brandy
1 tbsp freshly chopped tarragon
1 tbsp freshly chopped parsley
1 tbsp double cream

Rub the inside of each mullet with a teaspoonful of salt, scrubbing hard to remove any discoloured membranes inside. Rinse thoroughly, then place a sprig of fresh tarragon inside each fish. Using a sharp knife, cut 2 diagonal slits on the side of each fish – this helps to speed even cooking.

Mix the vegetable oil, tarragon vinegar and a little salt and pepper together in a small bowl. Arrange the fish in a shallow dish and pour the tarragon vinegar marinade over, brushing some of the mixture into the cuts on the sides of the fish. Refrigerate for 30 minutes.

Place the egg in a liquidiser or food processor with the mustard and a little salt and pepper. Blend for 2-3 seconds to mix then, with the machine running, add the oil through the feed-tube in a thin, steady stream. Continue blending the dressing until it is thick and creamy. Add the wine vinegar, brandy and herbs, and process for a further 30 seconds to mix well. Lightly whip the cream with a small whisk until it thickens. Fold the cream carefully into the oil and vinegar dressing. Pour into a serving dish and refrigerate until ready to use.

Arrange the fish on a grill pan and cook under a pre-heated grill for 5-8 minutes per side, depending on the size of the fish. Baste frequently with the marinade during cooking, then serve with a little of the sauce and some sprigs of fresh tarragon.

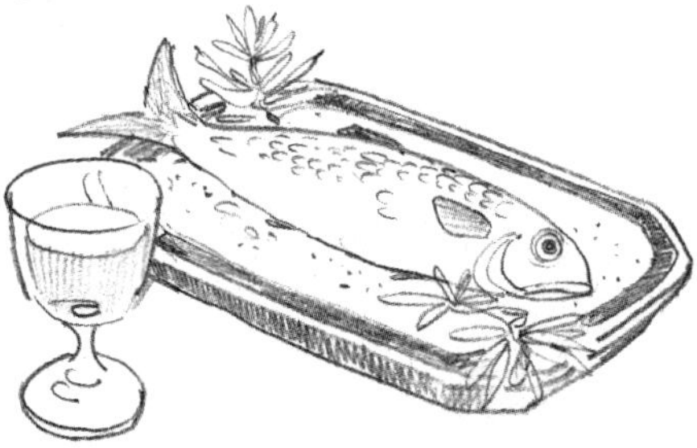

RED MULLET WITH HERBS 'EN PAPILLOTE'

Cooking 'en papillote' means cooking in a parcel, with the food wrapped up to keep it moist in its juices. Greaseproof paper is the most traditional wrapping, although foil can also be used. Greaseproof looks good and the food is often presented at the table still wrapped – foil is not so attractive and should be removed before serving.

Serves 4

Ingredients

Oil
4 red mullet, gutted and trimmed
60g/2oz butter
3 shallots, finely chopped
4 tbsps freshly chopped herbs such as chervil, tarragon, marjoram, basil and parsley
Salt and freshly ground black pepper
4 tbsps dry white wine
Lemon wedges or slices for garnish

Preheat the oven to 180°C/350°F/Gas Mark 4. Cut 4 circles of greaseproof paper or foil large enough to enclose the fish. Brush the circles with oil and place a fish on the lower half of each. Melt the butter in a small pan, add the shallots and cook until lightly browned, then add the herbs and salt and pepper. Pour 1 tablespoon of wine over each fish, then spoon the butter mixture over. Fold the greaseproof paper or foil over the mullet and seal the ends. Place the papillotes in a roasting tin or on a baking sheet with a lip around the edge, in case the parcels leak.

Cook the red mullet in the preheated oven for about 20-25 minutes – the cooking time will vary according to the size of the fish. Place the parcels on individual serving plates and allow each person to open their own. Serve with lemon wedges.

SWORDFISH STEAKS WITH GREEN PEPPERCORNS AND GARLIC SAUCE

Swordfish is a very meaty fish, slightly pink in colour when raw but white when cooked. It is inclined to dryness so the best way to prepare swordfish is by marinating it. This recipe grills the steaks – they also barbecue well. The garlic sauce served with the swordfish is an aïoli, a rich garlic mayonnaise.

Serves 4

INGREDIENTS
2 tbsps green peppercorns
6 tbsps lemon juice
4 tbsps olive oil
Freshly ground sea salt
4 swordfish steaks

Aïoli
1 egg
1 clove garlic, roughly chopped
150ml/¼ pint oil
2 tsps freshly chopped oregano
Freshly ground black pepper

Crush the green peppercorns lightly using a pestle and mortar, then mix them with the lemon juice, olive oil and salt. Place the swordfish steaks in a shallow ovenproof dish and pour the lemon and oil mixture over the fish, coating each steak. Refrigerate for 6-8 hours or overnight, turning occasionally, until the fish becomes opaque.

To make the aïoli, blend the egg and garlic together in a liquidiser or food processor. With the motor running, gradually add the oil through the feed tube in a thin, steady stream. Continue to blend until the sauce is thick.

Preheat the grill until very hot and arrange the swordfish in the grill pan. Sprinkle the chopped oregano over the swordfish steaks and season well. Cook for 15 minutes, turning frequently and basting with the lemon and pepper marinade.

Arrange the cooked swordfish steaks on a warmed serving dish and spoon the aïoli over to serve.

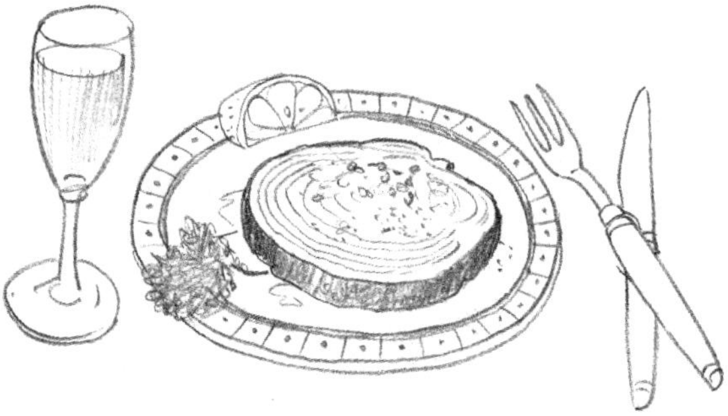

CRISPY GRIDDLED MACKEREL

Mackerel is a rich, flavoursome fish – a common catch along the north coast of France. It benefits the simplest of cooking – pan frying or cooking on a hot griddle.

Serves 4-8

INGREDIENTS
8 medium-sized fresh mackerel, gutted, washed and wiped dry
120g/4oz plain flour
150ml/¼ pint oil
Salt

To Serve
2 lemons, cut into quarters
2 tbsps freshly chopped parsley

Make sure the mackerel are really dry: use absorbent kitchen paper to soak up every last drop of water. Preheat a griddle or frying pan until very hot. Roll each fish in the flour, shaking off any excess, then dip the floured fish into the oil, and sprinkle with the salt. Place them on the griddle or frying pan and cook until crisp – this takes about 15 minutes if the mackerel are of average thickness. Turn the fish once during cooking – do not attempt this before the mackerel are ready and will release from the surface easily, otherwise they will stick and the presentation will be spoilt. Sprinkle with salt and chopped parsley before serving.

GOUJONS OF SOLE

The term 'goujon' is applied to small pieces of fish, coated in breadcrumbs and fried. Sole is the fish most frequently served in this way. The curry and tomato sauces give an excellent variety of dips for serving with the sole.

Serves 4

INGREDIENTS
2 lemon soles, filleted and skinned
Seasoned flour
1 egg, lightly beaten
2 tsps olive oil
Dry breadcrumbs
Oil for deep-frying
Pinch of salt
Lemon wedges

Tartare Sauce
2 tbsps mayonnaise
1 tbsp double cream
2 tsps freshly chopped parsley
2 tsps chopped gherkins
2 tsps chopped capers
1 tsp chopped onion

Curry Sauce
2 tbsps mayonnaise
1 tbsp double cream
1 tsp curry paste
1½ tsps mango chutney

Tomato Herb Sauce
2 tbsps mayonnaise
1 tbsp double cream
1 tsp freshly chopped parsley
1 tsp freshly chopped chives
1 tsp tomato purée
Lemon juice

Cut the sole fillets on the diagonal into pieces about 1.25cm/½ inch thick and 6-7.5cm/2½-3 inches long. Coat the fish thoroughly in seasoned flour, then shake to remove any excess. Beat the egg lightly with the olive oil.

Prepare the various sauces simply by combining the ingredients together. Place in small serving dishes and set aside until the sole is cooked.

Heat some oil in a deep-fryer to 190°C/375°F. Dip the floured fish in the beaten egg then coat the fish pieces in the breadcrumbs. Lower the goujons into the oil in a wire basket and cook until crisp and golden in 2-3 minutes. Cook the sole in two or three batches to prevent the pieces sticking together during cooking.

Drain the cooked fish on absorbent kitchen paper, then sprinkle lightly with salt and pile into a hot serving dish. Continue frying until all the sole is cooked, then serve, garnished with parsley and lemon wedges, with the sauces handed separately for dipping.

TRUITE EN PAPILLOTE

Cooking 'en papillote' is a simple but effective way of preparing fish, keeping it moist during cooking and giving an attractive style of presentation. Foil may be used in place of greaseproof but I don't think that it is so attractive for serving so I would recommend that you unwrap the fish in the kitchen if you do use foil.

Serves 4

INGREDIENTS

4 small trout, cleaned, each about 225g/8oz in weight
Salt and freshly ground black pepper
Sprigs of rosemary
2–3 shallots
120g/4oz butter
Lemon juice
120g/4oz flaked almonds
Lemon slices to garnish

Preheat the oven to 180°C/350°F/Gas mark 4. Trim the fins of the trout and lightly season the cavities, placing a small sprig of rosemary in each, and making two or three slits in each side of each fish to speed cooking. Finely chop the shallots and melt half the butter.

Cut four large circles of greaseproof paper, brush them with the butter and place a fish on each. Scatter the trout with the shallots, a little salt and pepper and some lemon juice, then pour the melted butter over the fish. Fold the paper up over the trout and seal well. Place the parcels on a baking sheet and bake in the preheated oven for 10–15 minutes.

Brown the almonds in the remaining butter, adding salt, pepper and a good squeeze of lemon juice. Add a little freshly chopped rosemary to the almonds just before serving.

Serve each trout in its parcel, slightly opened, and with a little of the hot butter and almonds spooned over the fish. Garnish with lemon slices.

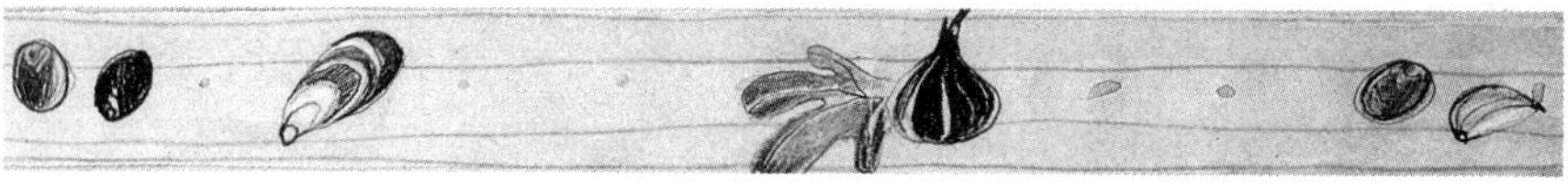

SEA BREAM WITH PEPPERCORN SAUCE

Filleting fish is easy to do at home, provided you have a sharp knife. Your fishmonger will, however, be happy to fillet the fish for you. I leave the skin on the fillets when grilling them, as it makes the fish easier to turn, with less risk of it breaking up.

Serves 6

INGREDIENTS
2 large sea bream, filleted
1 tbsp olive oil
10 green peppercorns
1 tbsp Cognac
2 shallots, skinned and finely chopped
1 tomato, seeded and chopped
1 sherry glass of Noilly Pratt
150ml/¼ pint white wine
1 tbsp sugar
225ml/8fl oz double cream
Salt

Fillet the bream, then set them to one side. Heat the olive oil in a frying pan and sauté the peppercorns for about 1 minute. Pour off the oil, add the Cognac and cook until almost evaporated. Add the shallots, tomato, Noilly Pratt, white wine and the sugar. Stir well and allow the mixture to thicken until quite syrupy. This may take quite a while if the tomato is very juicy. Whilst the sauce is thickening, cook the fish fillets under a hot grill – this will take 4-5 minutes. Stir the cream into the sauce over a very gentle heat, ensuring that the sauce does not boil. Season with salt. Blend the sauce until smooth in a liquidiser or food processor and serve poured over the hot fish.

SOLE AU VIN ROUGE
SOLE IN RED WINE

Sole is most usually cooked in a white wine sauce and served with white grapes, but red wine makes a very pleasant, and surprisingly delicious, change. Use a light red wine, a Bordeaux would work well.

Serves 4

INGREDIENTS

2 whole lemon or Dover sole, filleted
150ml/¼ pint red wine
75ml/2½fl oz water
1 slice onion
3-4 peppercorns
1 bay leaf
1 small bunch black grapes
15g/½oz butter
15g/½oz flour
150ml/¼ pint double cream
Salt and freshly ground black pepper

Preheat the oven to 160°C/325°F/Gas Mark 3. Skin the fish fillets, then fold the thin ends of the fillets under to make neat parcels of uniform thickness. Place in an ovenproof dish and pour the wine and water over the fillets. Add the onion, peppercorns, bay leaf and a pinch of salt, then cover the dish with foil. Bake in the preheated oven for about 10 minutes.

Wash the grapes and remove the seeds – leave the grapes whole unless they are very large, in which case they should be cut in half.

Remove the sole from the baking dish, cover and keep warm. Strain and reserve the cooking liquor. Melt the butter in a small pan until foaming, then remove the pan from the heat and stir in the flour. Return to the heat and cook for 2-3 minutes, stirring all the time, until lightly browned. Gradually whisk in the fish liquor and heat, stirring all the time, until the sauce boils and thickens. Add the cream and boil again, then season to taste. Add most of the grapes and heat gently.

Arrange the fillets of sole in a serving dish, then spoon the sauce over. Garnish with the remaining grapes before serving.

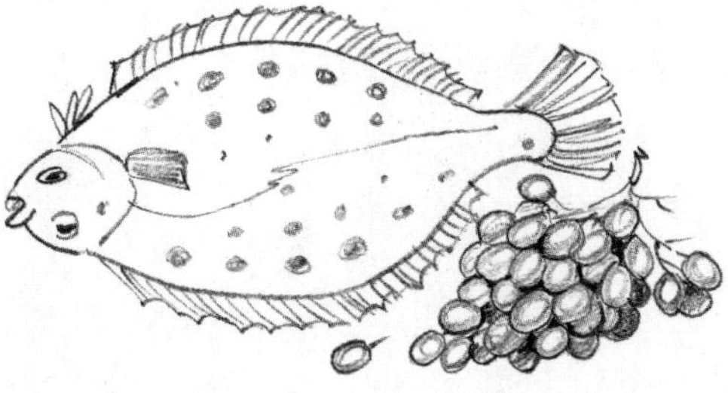

BRANDADE DE MORUE
CREAMED SALT COD

Salt cod is used throughout France, although it usually comes from Brittany or from the Breton fisherman who bring it from Iceland. It was a valuable winter food in years gone by, before refrigeration. Poach the cod slowly or it may become stringy. Serve with bread or garlic bread and a tomato garnish.

Serves 6

INGREDIENTS
1kg/2¼lbs salt cod
430ml/¾ pint olive oil
280ml/½ pint double cream
Freshly ground black pepper

Soak the cod for one day in cold water, changing the water frequently to remove the excess salt. Poach the fish in a pan of water for 7 minutes, then drain well. Remove all the bones and the skin, and flake the fish very finely.

In a large saucepan, gently heat about one quarter of the oil and add the fish, stirring and mixing well until a fine paste is achieved. Remove from the heat and, using a spatula, briskly work in the remaining oil and the cream, adding them alternately, little by little. Season well with pepper.

GRIDDLED TUNA STEAKS

Fresh tuna is widely available in supermarkets and fishmongers. It can be dry if over-cooked and is really at its best when cooked rare, still slightly pink and moist in the centre.

Serves 6

INGREDIENTS
6 fresh tuna steaks
4 tbsps olive oil
2 tbsps freshly chopped mixed herbs

Dressing
1 tomato
1 tbsp vinegar
2 tbsps olive oil
1 tbsp freshly chopped herbs
Salt and freshly ground black pepper

Remove the bones from the tuna, shape the fish into circles and secure around the egdes with kitchen string. Place on a shallow plate and coat with the olive oil, then sprinkle with the herbs. Place in the refrigerator for at least 3 hours.

Preheat a griddle, frying pan or barbeque until very hot and cook the fish until crispy on the outside and just slightly pink in the centre – this will take 8-10 minutes. Skin the tomato and chop it into small dice. Make a vinaigrette by mixing together the vinegar, oil and the herbs. Season well with salt and pepper. Stir in the tomato and serve with of the fish.

ROLLED SOLE FILLETS

This is the classic way to prepare fillets of sole although the stuffing may vary according to season and personal choice. The rich, creamy sauce helps to complete a classic dish.

Serves 6

INGREDIENTS
6 medium sole fillets, halved lengthways
2 tbsps freshly chopped herbs, (parsley, chives, basil, etc.)
570ml/1 pint fish stock
225g/8oz mushrooms, chopped
1 clove garlic, chopped
280ml/½ pint double cream
Salt and freshly ground black pepper

Beat the sole fillets until flat; place them between 2 sheets of waxed paper or plastic wrap, and flatten with light strokes of a rolling pin. Sprinkle the fresh herbs over the fish and then roll up the fillets and secure with wooden cocktail sticks.

Boil the stock in a saucepan over a high heat and allow it to reduce by half. Add the mushrooms and garlic and cook for 8 minutes. Remove from the heat, beat in the cream and add a little salt and pepper. Remove the mushrooms with a slotted spoon and set them aside. Allow the stock to cool slightly, then blend until smooth in a liquidiser or food processor.

Meanwhile, steam the fish rolls until cooked – this will take about 8 minutes. Return the mushrooms to the sauce and reheat but do not allow the sauce to boil. Serve the sole on a warmed serving dish with the sauce poured over.

GRILLED TROUT

This is a very easy recipe for cooking trout, and it follows the French philosophy of cooking prime ingredients in a very simple way to celebrate the flavour of the food. Use the roe from the trout, if possible, or soft herring roe, for garnish. Fry the roe, or heat through as necessary. The trout will take 15-20 minutes to cook, depending on size.

Serves 6

Ingredients

6 river trout, cleaned
2 tbsps olive oil
Salt and freshly ground black pepper
Juice of 1 lemon
120g/4oz fresh fish roe (lumpfish, keta or salmon trout), optional

Begin by preparing the trout. Cut off the fins, wash well under running water and dry them on absorbent kitchen paper. If using a grill, set it to high, or heat a flat griddle or frying pan. Dip the trout in the olive oil and sprinkle them with salt and pepper. Cook the fish until crispy on the outside and just tender on the inside – turn once, half way through cooking. Pour a little lemon juice over each fish and serve hot with a spoonful of fish roe if wished.

QUENELLES AU BEURRE BLANC

Quenelles are a classic dish – lightly poached mousses of pike served with a buttery sauce and vegetable garnish. They require careful preparation but are well worth the effort.

Serves 4

INGREDIENTS

Quenelles
460g/1lb pike or other white fish
120g/4oz white breadcrumbs
4 tbsps milk
90g/3oz butter
2 eggs
Salt and white pepper
Nutmeg
Cayenne Pepper

Beurre Blanc Sauce
1 small onion, finely chopped
1 tbsp white wine vinegar
3 tbsps dry white wine
120g/4oz unsalted butter, cut into small pieces
Salt
2 tbsps lemon juice
1 tsp freshly chopped chives

Vegetable Garnish
1 carrot, peeled
1 stick celery, trimmed
1 medium courgette, trimmed
1 leek, trimmed, with some green attached

First prepare the quenelle mixture. Skin and bone the fish and cut it into small pieces. Soak the breadcrumbs in the milk for a few minutes, then drain away most of the liquid and place the breadcrumbs and fish in a food processor. Melt the butter then pour it into the fish mixture with the machine running. Process to a smooth purée then add the eggs and seasonings. Chill the quenelle mixture in the refrigerator for at least one hour.

Prepare the vegetable garnish. Cut all the vegetables into 5cm/2inch lengths, then cut those into thin julienne strips. Bring a large saucepan of salted water to the boil, add the carrots and cook for 3 minutes. Add the celery and cook for a further 5 minutes then finally add the courgette and leek and cook for a further 3 minutes.

While the vegetables are cooking bring a sauté pan of lightly salted water to the boil. Using two dessert spoons shape the chilled fish mixture into small oval shapes. Poach the quenelles in the simmering water for 6 minutes, turning them over once during cooking. Remove the quenelles from the pan with a slotted spoon, drain and place in a covered dish in a low oven to keep warm.

To prepare the sauce, place the onion in a small pan with the vinegar and wine. Boil until reduced by half, then remove the pan from the heat and allow to cool slightly. Add a few pieces of butter, whisking well to give a smooth creamy sauce. Return the pan to the heat, gradually adding the remaining butter and whisking all the time. Season the sauce, add the lemon juice and then strain the sauce through a fine sieve. Adjust the seasoning then add the drained vegetable garnish and the freshly chopped chives.

Serve the quenelles with the beurre blanc sauce poured over.

MACKEREL WITH PEPPERCORNS

Smoked fish is very popular in France, and so are vinaigrette dressings. Combine the two and you have a most delicious but simple salad. The strong flavour of the mackerel is complemented by a well-flavoured dressing.

Serves 6

INGREDIENTS

1 tbsp wine vinegar
Salt and freshly ground black pepper
3 tbsps olive oil
3 shallots, finely chopped
3 whole smoked mackerel with peppercorns, halved, or 6 smoked mackerel fillets
2 lollo-rosso lettuces, washed and dried
2 tomatoes, skinned, seeded and diced
2 sprigs of fresh fennel, snipped

Make the vinaigrette by beating together the vinegar, salt and pepper, oil and the shallots. Cut the mackerel into fairly thick slices. Place the prepared lettuce on a serving plate, add the slices of mackerel and pour the vinaigrette dressing over. Decorate the plate with the diced tomato and the snipped fennel sprigs, and serve immediately.

SCALLOPS WITH FRESH BASIL

This dish is so incredibly simple and so utterly luxurious! It is also quick. Do not attempt to prepare the scallops or the chicory in advance as they will spoil – this has to be prepared at the last moment.

Serves 4-6

INGREDIENTS
8 heads of chicory
120g/4oz butter
Salt and white pepper
2 cloves garlic, finely chopped
10 leaves fresh basil, finely chopped
18 large scallops, rinsed, dried and halved

Separate the chicory leaves and cut them lengthways into thin strips. Cook them in a frying pan in half the butter and a little salt and pepper until quite tender.

Melt the remaining butter in a clean frying pan, add the garlic and basil and cook for a few minutes. Turn the heat up to high and sauté the scallops for 1-2 minutes in the mixture, first on one side and then on the other, taking care not to overcook them. Add a little salt and pepper. Serve the scallops in their sauce on a bed of warm chicory.

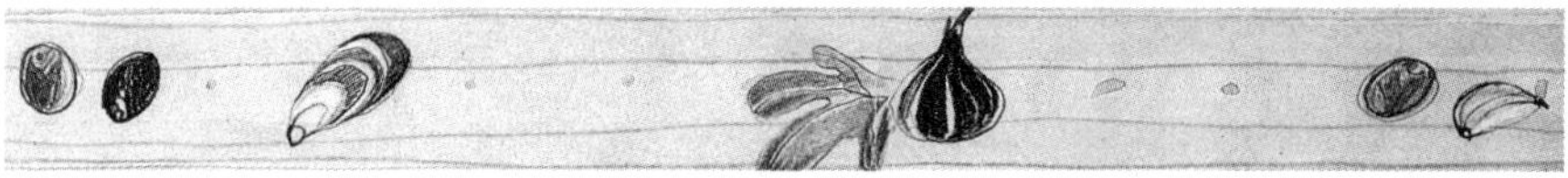

STUFFED SQUID

I have a passion for squid and enjoy cooking it in many different ways. Stuffing squid is not as complicated as it sounds – place the whiting mixture in a forcing bag fitted with a large plain nozzle and squeeze the stuffing into the squid!

Serves 2 as a light supper or 4 as a starter

INGREDIENTS

340g/¾lb whiting fillets, skinned
200ml/7fl oz single cream
1 egg, beaten
Salt and freshly ground black pepper
½ carrot, diced
½ courgette, peeled and diced
200ml/7fl oz double cream
4 medium squid, well rinsed and dried inside and out, tentacles cut off
570ml/1 pint fish stock
2 pinches of saffron

To make the stuffing, purée the whiting fillets with 1 tbsp single cream and the beaten egg in a liquidiser or food processor. Add salt and pepper. Blanch the carrot and courgette cubes in boiling water for 2 minutes and add to the whiting. Stir well to mix evenly, then whip the double cream and fold it into the fish stuffing.

Stuff the squid with the whiting mixture, forcing it well down the tubes. Sew the ends up with fine kitchen thread or string to enclose the stuffing. Steam the squid for 15-20 minutes. Heat the stock in a saucepan, allowing it to reduce by three-quarters. Stir in the remaining single cream and the saffron. Allow the sauce to heat through and then blend until smooth in a liquidiser or food processor.

Remove the string from the squid and serve with the sauce poured over.

MOULES MARINIÈRE

Moules Marinière, cooked in the style of the fisherman's wife, is one of the best-known of classic French dishes. It is simple to prepare but care must be taken not to overcook the mussels. Shake the pan frequently – this mixes them up and helps to prevent them from sticking.

Serves 4

INGREDIENTS
3 litres/5½ pints mussels, pre–soaked for 1 hour in salted water
60g/2oz butter
1 large onion, thinly sliced
2 cloves garlic, chopped
2 sprigs parsley
Salt and freshly ground black pepper
1.14 litres/2 pints dry white wine

To Serve
3 tbsps freshly chopped parsley

Drain the mussels. Scrape off any persistent scales and rinse the mussels thoroughly in cold running water. Remove any stringy beards. Melt half the butter in a large saucepan and cook the onion, garlic, sprigs of parsley, salt and pepper for 4 minutes. Pour in the wine and bring to the boil. Add the mussels, cover and cook for about 8 minutes, or until all the shells have opened. Take the saucepan off the heat and remove the mussels with a slotted spoon. Discard any that have not opened. Keep the mussels warm.

Remove the sprig of parsley from the cooking liquor and strain through a fine sieve. Return the liquor to the saucepan over a high heat and bring it to the boil. Boil to reduce by at least one third. Stir in the remaining butter and a little more salt and pepper to taste. Stir in the mussels and serve hot, sprinkled with chopped parsley.

SCALLOPS AU GRATIN

Scallops require very gentle cooking – overcooking will toughen them, making them unpleasant to eat, when they should be a delectable treat. Do not use frozen scallops – they are seldom little more than mush once thawed.

Serves 4 as a fish starter or 2 as a light supper

INGREDIENTS

4 large scallops
2 tbsps olive oil
60g/2oz butter
2 small shallots or 1 small onion, finely chopped
1 glass of white wine
2 tbsps double cream
2 egg yolks, lightly beaten
Salt and white pepper
45g/1½oz Cheddar cheese, grated
4 tbsps fresh white breadcrumbs

Allow one large scallop or two to three smaller scallops per person. Ask your fishmonger for four deep scallop shells in which to serve the starter.

Heat the oil and butter in a heavy frying pan, add the shallots and cook gently until soft. Slice the white of the scallops horizontally. Increase the heat, add the white wine then the sliced scallops and cook briskly for 2-3 minutes. Slice the scallop corals and add them to the pan, cooking for a further 1 minute. Remove the pan from the heat and allow to cool slightly.

Add the cream to the scallops then carefully stir in the lightly beaten egg yolks. Stir gently over a low heat until slightly thickened, then season lightly to taste. Divide the mixture between the scallop shells or four individual dishes, ensuring that each has a fair share of coral.

Mix the cheese and breadcrumbs together and divide the mixture between the dishes. Place under a hot grill until just beginning to brown. Serve the scallops immediately with brown bread and butter.

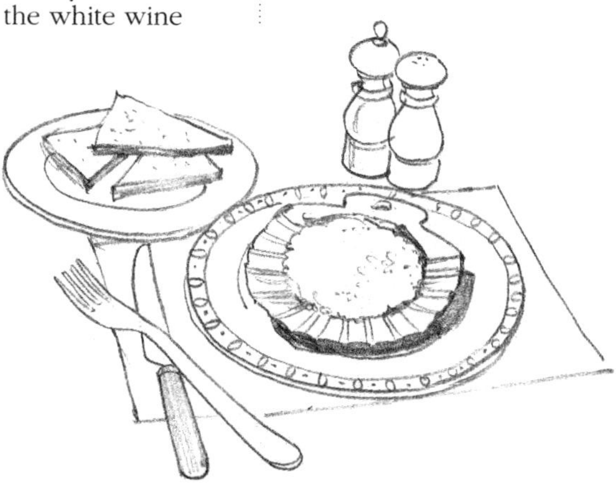

CALAMARS DE PROVENCE

I love squid, but many people who try it fried are put off, finding it chewy and tough. A slower cooking, such as in this recipe, helps to tenderise the squid – this is the way I like to cook it. I sometimes stew the squid for an hour or more – they don't spoil; I think they get better!

Serves 6

INGREDIENTS
Olive oil
2.3kg/5lbs squid tubes, washed and cut into thin slices
1 tsp fennel seeds (optional)
5 onions, chopped
5 cloves garlic, chopped
1 tsp cayenne pepper
1 bouquet garni
5 tomatoes, chopped
280ml/½ pint fish stock
280ml/½ pint dry white wine
Pinch of saffron
1 tbsp double cream
Salt and freshly ground black pepper

Warm the oil in a frying pan and cook the squid and fennel seeds until all the juices evaporate. Remove the squid with a slotted spoon and add the onion, garlic, cayenne pepper, bouquet garni and the tomatoes to the pan. Stir well and cook for a few minutes. Add the stock and the wine, sprinkle in the saffron and stir well. Cook over a fairly brisk heat until the sauce has reduced by half. Return the squid to the pan, reduce the heat, cover and cook very gently until the squid is tender – about 20 minutes. Just before serving, remove the bouquet garni and stir in the cream. Check the seasoning and add a little salt and pepper if necessary.

COQUILLES ST JACQUES

Scallops are a real treat. Frozen scallops look tempting until they defrost, at which stage they often go to a soggy mush. Fresh scallops are vastly superior in both flavour and texture. Have the potato and scallop mixtures hot before grilling, so that the potato can brown quickly and the scallops will not over-cook.

Serves 4

INGREDIENTS
8 large scallops, cleaned
280ml/½ pint dry white wine
460g/1lb potatoes
1 egg yolk
90g/3oz butter
Salt and pepper - I use white pepper with scallops
Half an onion, very finely chopped
120g/4oz mushrooms, sliced
40g/1½oz flour
150ml/¼ pint double cream
Sprig of thyme
1 tbsp freshly chopped parsley
60g/2oz shelled prawns

4 scallop shells for serving

Remove and reserve the orange corals from the scallops. Slice the white parts into rounds and poach them gently in the dry white wine for 3-4 minutes (do not overcook the scallops or they will become tough and rubbery). Strain the scallops, reserving the liquid. Whilst the scallops are poaching, boil the potatoes in salted water until soft. Drain and mash the potatoes, adding the egg yolk, 25g/1oz of the butter and seasonings. Set aside until required.

Melt the remaining 60g/2oz of butter in a small saucepan, add the chopped onion and cook for 2 minutes. Add the mushrooms and cook for a further 5 minutes or so. Sprinkle in the flour and cook, stirring all the time, for 1 minute, then gradually add the scallop liquor, a little at a time. Mix to a smooth sauce and cook for 2-3 minutes over a gentle heat before adding the double cream and herbs. Season to taste and add the prawns and scallop corals. Heat gently until almost boiling, then remove the thyme and divide the mixture between the 4 scallop shells.

Pipe a little of the creamed potato around the edge of each scallop shell. Preheat the grill, then place the shells on the grill pan and cook until the potato is lightly golden. Serve immediately.

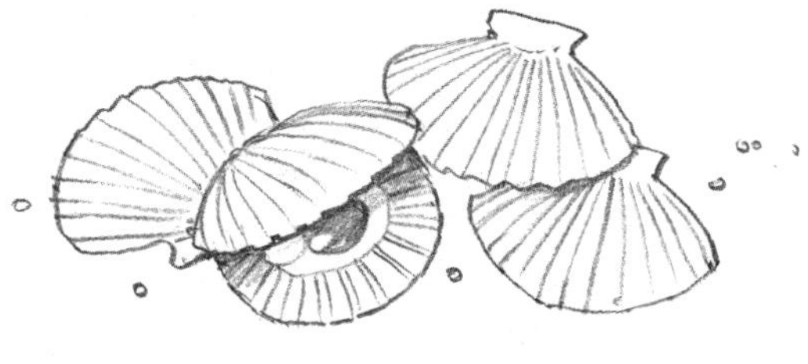

SOUFFLÉS ST JACQUES

These scallop soufflés combine two great traditions of French cuisine! Served with a tomato sauce, they both look and taste good!

Serves 4

Ingredients

8 large or 16 small scallops, with roe attached
280ml/½ pint milk
45g/1½oz butter
45g/1½oz flour
Salt and white pepper
¼ tsp Dijon mustard
45g/1½oz grated Cheddar cheese
4 eggs, separated

Tomato Sauce

400g/14oz can of tomatoes
1 small onion, finely chopped
Bay leaf
Pinch of thyme
Sugar to taste
Half a clove of garlic, crushed
1 tbsp Worcestershire sauce
Salt and white pepper

Prepare the tomato sauce. Place all the ingredients in a small, heavy-based saucepan and bring to the boil. Simmer, half covered, for 20 minutes, then strain the sauce through a sieve and set it to one side.

Preheat the oven to 230°C/450°F/Gas Mark 8. Poach the scallops in the milk for 3-5 minutes, depending on size. Remove the scallops from the milk and set aside. Melt the butter in a pan until foaming, remove from the heat and beat in the flour. Cook gently for about 1 minute, but do not allow the mixture to brown. Gradually beat in the milk in which the scallops were poached. Bring the mixture slowly to the boil, stirring all the time, and cook until thickened. Add the salt and pepper, mustard and grated cheese, then allow the mixture to cool slightly, before beating in the egg yolks.

Butter 4 ramekins or shell dishes. Slice the scallops horizontally reserving 4 whole roes for garnish and place the scallops in the bottom of the dishes. Whisk the egg whites until stiff but not dry and fold them into the cheese mixture. Spoon the soufflé into the prepared dishes and place them on a baking sheet. Bake in the preheated oven for about 10 minutes, or until well risen and set.

Reheat the tomato sauce whilst the soufflés are baking and serve a little spooned over each soufflé, garnished with the reserved roes. Serve any remaining tomato sauce with the soufflés.

LOBSTER À LA CRÈME

This is a good way of making one lobster go a long way! A very rich and luxurious dish. Try using Calvados in place of the sherry.

Serves 2

Ingredients

1 cold, boiled lobster
90g/3oz butter
Salt and freshly ground black pepper
Squeeze of lemon juice
Freshly grated nutmeg
1 small bunch tarragon, chopped
75ml/2½fl oz dry sherry or Madeira
280ml/½ pint double cream
3 tbsps dry white breadcrumbs

Use a sharp knife to cut the lobster in half lengthways. Remove all the meat from the tail, crack the claws and remove the meat from them then extract as much as possible from the legs. Chop all the meat roughly.

Melt 60g/2oz of the butter in a pan and sauté the lobster with the seasonings, lemon juice, nutmeg and tarragon. Add the sherry or Madeira to the pan, heat and flame, shaking the pan until the flames die out.

Add the cream to the pan, and bring it to the boil, then boil for 5 minutes or until the cream begins to thicken. Spoon the lobster cream into 2 individual dishes and keep warm.

Melt the remaining butter in a small pan, add the breadcrumbs and fry until browned. Scatter the breadcrumbs over the lobster creams and serve.

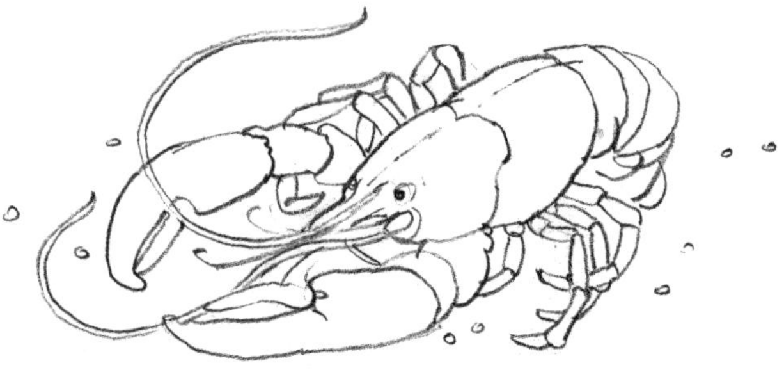

HARLEQUIN SCALLOPS

This particularly attractive dish is perfect for a special occasion. Take care when preparing the vegetables, they should be cut into very small cubes (brunaise). This way they remain quite crisp during cooking. The vegetables and scallops should be cooked over a very gentle heat. Queen scallops, or queenies, are very small, about 7cm/3 inches in diameter. Use if available and serve in ordinary-sized scallop shells for an attractive finish.

Serves 6

INGREDIENTS

54 fresh Queen scallops (or 24 ordinary-sized scallops), on the half-shell
2 tbsps olive oil
1 clove garlic, finely chopped
1 red pepper, seeded and cut into small dice
1 green pepper, seeded and cut into small dice
1 stick celery, cut into small cubes
2 carrots, peeled and cut into small cubes
Salt and freshly ground black pepper
1 pinch of thyme

Preheat the oven to 200°C/400°F/Gas mark 6. Slide all the scallops on to a plate. Keep cool.

Warm the oil in a large frying pan, with the garlic, and add all the vegetables and the scallops. Cook in batches if necessary. Add a little salt and pepper and the thyme. Cook very gently for a few minutes, stirring frequently, until the scallops are just done. (Opaque but slightly transparent in the centre). The exact cooking time will depend on quantity and size. After cooking, the vegetables should still be quite crisp. Fill 36 (or 24) ordinary-sized scallop shells with a little of the mixture and then put them in the hot oven for 5 minutes or so, to cook through completely. Serve piping hot.

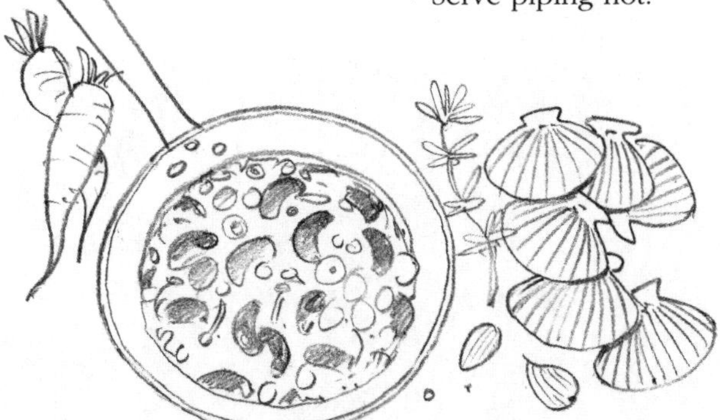

CRAB SALAD WITH RUM

A light salad with the Spanish influence of rum. This is best made with fresh crab meat; canned crab is suitable for use when fresh crabs are out of season.

Serves 6

INGREDIENTS

Juice of 2 lemons
2 avocados
4 artichoke hearts
1 head lettuce, washed, dried and shredded
3 sticks celery, wiped, strings removed and sliced
340g/¾lb fresh crab meat

Sauce

1 egg yolk
2 tsps Dijon mustard
150ml/¼ pint oil
4 tbsps single cream
3 tbsps rum
1 tbsp freshly chopped parsley
Salt and freshly ground black pepper

Have the lemon juice ready. Peel the avocados and, with a melon baller, scoop out the flesh. Dip the balls immediately into the lemon juice, then place them in a bowl in the refrigerator. Dice the artichoke hearts and dip them into the lemon juice, then place them in the refrigerator with the avocado balls.

Make the sauce by beating the egg yolk with the mustard. Beat in the oil, drop by drop, then beat in the cream, rum, parsley, salt and pepper.

Place a small bed of lettuce on 6 individual plates, and top with the avocado, artichoke and the celery. Break up the crab meat and scatter it over the salad. Serve with the rum sauce spooned over.

SALADE AUX FRUITS DE MER

This is a celebration of sea food! It can be made with any combination of fish, but use a mixture of shellfish and white fish. Cook and eat the salad on the same day.

Serves 4

INGREDIENTS

Salad

8 scallops with roe attached
175g/6oz monkfish
Lemon juice
Mussels
Cooked scampi
Cooked, peeled prawns
1 head of lettuce
1 head of chicory

Dressing

120g/4oz curd cheese
150ml/¼ pint yogurt
Juice of 1 lemon
3 tbsps milk
1 tbsp Dijon mustard
1 tbsp freshly chopped tarragon
1 tbsp freshly chopped chives
1 tbsp freshly chopped parsley
Salt and freshly ground black pepper

Poach the scallops and monkfish in a large pan in a little lemon juice with enough water to cover the fish. Cook for 5 minutes, then add the mussels, cover and cook for a further 3-4 minutes, until the mussels have opened. Remove all the fish from the pan and allow it to cool completely. Add the scampi and prawns. Chill.

Prepare the dressing by whisking all the ingredients together. Arrange the lettuce and chicory on a large platter and top with the chilled mixed fish. Spoon the dressing over and serve immediately.

POULTRY & GAME

I actually find that I cannot go along with the traditional French country attitude towards poultry and game; well, that is until it reaches the kitchen work surface! Although I love the markets in towns and villages for fresh fruits and vegetables I find the poultry stalls just a little too fresh – the birds are usually still alive! The stall holder might wring the bird's neck but you will usually have to do the rest of the work yourself. I am afraid that, although I love food and thoroughly enjoy cooking, this is really too much for me and I would rather pay the premium for a corn-fed, oven-ready chicken than pluck and draw a bird myself. There, underneath it all I'm just another sentimental Brit!

Fresh Is Best

Of course, buying in the French way does ensure that poultry is as fresh as possible which is very important and a matter of great pride to the housewife and cook. The age of a bird in feather can easily be determined by feeling the beak – in a young bird it will be flexible, a good indication that the bird will be tender. Game birds, such as partridge and pheasants, need to be hung to develop their flavour.

An Empty Canvass

The marvellous thing about poultry, and especially chicken, is that it so readily accepts the flavours of other ingredients that are cooked with it. The great French gastronome Brillat-Savarin wrote that "Poultry is for the cook what canvas is to the painter" and so it is, the starting-off point, the main ingredient of so many great and classic dishes. Some even relate to events in French history; Chicken Marengo was – so popular legend has it – created by Napoleon's chef to celebrate his victory against the Austrians at the Battle of Marengo. The battle was actually fought in Italy, just north of Genoa, so this classic French dish was first created from ingredients that were readily available in the Italian countryside; chicken, tomatoes, sherry or marsala, mushrooms, and eggs.

From the New World to the Old

Although I know that the French for turkey is *dindon*, I can actually think of very few classic French recipes which feature this bird. However, it must be popular in France as Brillat-Savarin described the turkey as "one of the finest gifts given to the Old World by the New." Escoffier described a meal of cream of pumpkin soup followed by young spit-roasted turkey served with a large country sausage, enjoyed after a day's hunting. Perhaps this in itself epitomises the French attitude to fine food, that the best and freshest ingredients need little embellishment and only simple dressing to make a truly memorable meal.

Duck or Duckling?

Nantais and Rouennais are to the French what Aylesbury is to the British – the best duck raised for the table! As duck can be somewhat fatty it is often cooked with fruit to lighten the richness of the meat; duck with orange, duck with tart black cherries, duck with apples and calvados. These dishes all stem from different regions of France; the south west is home to the cherries, Normandy to apples, and this local association of ingredients can be seen in all the cookery of France. And when is a duck not a duck? When it's a duckling, and that is only for the first two months of its life. Duckling does not have the same gamy flavour as duck and is best simply roasted.

Goose – the Gourmet's Delight

'Hissing and honking' is a colourful description of geese in a farmyard, and really very accurate! The ideal holiday image of a rural scene in south west France, the main goose and foie gras area, is bound to feature geese in abundance. The meat itself is enjoyed casseroled or slowly roasted but it is the liver, the *foie gras*, which is the delicacy of France.

Pheasant and Partridge – Real Country Cooking

The French country people eat a lot of game birds; pheasant, partridge, pigeon and woodcock. In the autumn the men disappear for *La Palombière*, a weekend or longer of elaborate pigeon shooting involving decoys and many bottles of wine!

It is the wine produced in France which gives so much regional flavour to the country dishes based on game. 'When in France, do as the French' – use the local wine to marinade the game birds as all will be redolent of the area, blending the local produce together, however simply cooked, in the most spectacular way.

SLICED CHICKEN WITH FIGS

A new recipe that presents chicken in a new light – this recipe will delight all who taste it. Serve with Rice Pilaf.

Serves 6

INGREDIENTS

60g/2oz butter
1 large chicken, boned and cut into slices
1 small cinnamon stick
280ml/½ pint white wine
280ml/½ pint chicken stock
Pinch of saffron
15 coriander seeds
6 dried figs, each cut into 3
2 tsps honey
Salt and freshly ground black pepper

In a heavy frying pan, melt the butter and the oil and fry the chicken slices. Allow to brown slightly, then take the pan off the heat. Remove the chicken from the frying pan and keep it warm. Put the frying pan back on the heat and add the cinnamon, wine, stock, saffron, coriander, figs, honey, salt and pepper. Stir well and cook for 4 minutes. Return the chicken to the frying pan, cover, and continue cooking for 20 minutes over a very gentle heat. Remove the chicken and the figs and keep them warm. Remove and discard the cinnamon. Allow the sauce to boil until quite syrupy. Return the chicken and the figs to the frying pan, heat through and serve.

GRILLED CHICKEN WITH LIME

A perfect summer dish combining the refreshing tang of limes with the lightness of chicken. This recipe gives instructions for grilling the chicken and finishing it in the oven, but it could easily be barbecued if preferred.

Serves 4

INGREDIENTS
2 x 900g/2lb chickens
Salt and freshly ground black pepper
1 tbsp freshly chopped basil
90ml/3fl oz olive oil
4 limes
Sugar to taste

Remove the leg and wing tips from the chickens and discard them. Split the chicken in half, cutting away the backbone completely and discarding it. Bend the chicken legs back to loosen the ball and socket joints and flatten each half of the chickens by hitting it with the flat side of a cleaver or a rolling pin. Season the chicken on both sides with salt and pepper and sprinkle with the basil. Place the chicken halves in a shallow dish and pour over 2 tbsps of olive oil. Squeeze the juice from 2 of the limes over the chicken, then cover the dish and leave the chicken to marinate in the refrigerator for 4 hours.

Heat the grill to its highest setting and preheat the oven to 190°C/375°F/Gas Mark 5. Remove the chicken from the marinade and place it in the grill pan. Cook one side until golden brown then turn the pieces over. Drizzle with 1 tbsp of olive oil and brown the other side.

Place the chicken in a roasting tin, drizzle with the remaining oil and roast in the preheated oven for about 25 minutes. Peel the remaining limes and slice them thinly. When the chicken is cooked, place the lime slices on top of the chicken and sprinkle with a little sugar. Place under a hot grill for a few minutes to caramelise the sugar and cook the limes. Transfer to a warmed serving dish. Heat any remaining marinade and the cooking juices together briefly, then spoon the juices over the chicken and serve immediately.

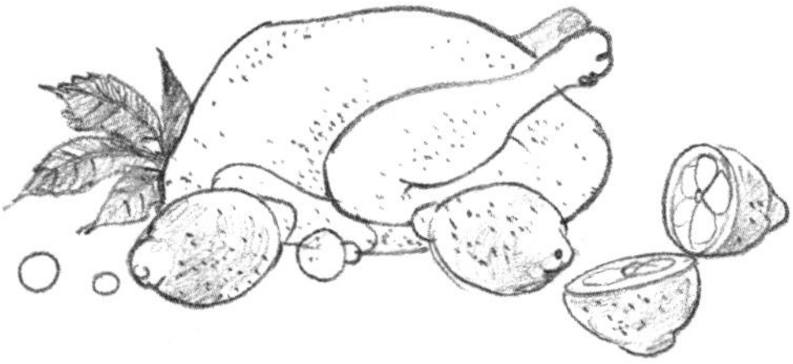

CHICKEN PROVENÇALE

A classic dish from Provençe in the south of France. The chicken is cooked with herbs, tomatoes, garlic, olives and anchovies for the authentic flavour of the Mediterranean.

Serves 4

INGREDIENTS
1 tsp salt
1 tsp black pepper
1 clove garlic, crushed
3 tbsps olive oil
1.8kg/4lb chicken, jointed into 8 pieces
1 medium onion, finely chopped
225g/8oz cup mushrooms, halved
30g/1oz flour
175ml/6fl oz white wine
120ml/4fl oz chicken stock
3 tomatoes, skinned, seeded and roughly chopped
1 tbsp fresh basil leaves, torn
6 black olives, halved and pitted
60g/2oz can anchovy fillets

Preheat the oven to 160°C/325°F/Gas Mark 3. Rub the salt, pepper and crushed garlic over the chicken pieces and set them aside. Heat the oil in a large flame-proof casserole and, when hot, sauté the chicken pieces, turning them frequently, until they are evenly browned. Reduce the heat, add the chopped onion and cook, covered, for about 20-25 minutes, until the chicken is tender. Remove the chicken to an ovenproof casserole and keep it warm in the oven whilst making the sauce.

Halve the mushrooms, add them to the original casserole and sauté for 2-3 minutes. Stir in the flour and cook for 30 seconds before gradually pouring in the wine and stock. Bring the sauce to the boil, stirring constantly. Add the tomatoes, basil and olives. Chop half the anchovies and add them to the casserole. Return the mixture to the boil, then reduce the heat and simmer for 10 minutes. Remove the chicken from the oven and coat it with the sauce, then garnish with the halved anchovies. Serve immediately.

POULET SAUTÉ VALLÉE D'AUGE
NORMANDY-STYLE CHICKEN

This is a classic dish of Normandy - chicken in a rich creamy sauce flavoured with apples and calvados, the famed apple brandy of the region. The chicken is garnished in a traditional way, with caramelised apple slices.

Serves 4

INGREDIENTS
60g/2oz butter
2 tbsps oil
1.4kg/3lbs chicken, jointed into eight pieces
4 tbsps Calvados
6 tbsps chicken stock
2 apples, peeled, cored and roughly chopped
1 shallot, finely chopped
2 sticks celery, finely chopped
1 tsp freshly chopped thyme
2 egg yolks, lightly beaten
90ml/3fl oz double cream
Salt and white pepper

Garnish
30g/1oz butter
2 apples, quartered, cored and diced
Sugar
1 bunch watercress or small parsley sprigs

Heat half the butter and all of the oil in a large sauté pan over a moderate heat. When the foam begins to subside, add the chicken, a few pieces at a time, and brown on all sides – place the chicken skin side down first. When all the chicken is browned, remove it from the pan, drain off most of the fat then return the chicken to the pan.

Pour the Calvados into a small saucepan and warm it gently over a low heat. Ignite it with a match and pour it, while still flaming, over the chicken. Shake the pan gently until the flames subside. If the calvados should flare up, cover the pan immediately with a lid. Pour in the stock and scrape any browned chicken juices up from the bottom of the pan. Set the chicken aside.

Melt the remaining butter in a small saucepan or frying pan. Cook the chopped apples, shallot and celery and the thyme for about 10 minutes or until soft but not browned. Spoon the mixture over the chicken and return the pan to a high heat. Bring to the boil, then reduce the heat, cover the pan and simmer for 50 minutes.

Beat the egg yolks and cream together and, with a whisk, gradually beat in some of the hot sauce from the chicken. Pour the mixture back into a saucepan and cook over a low heat for 2-3 minutes, stirring constantly, until the sauce thickens and coats the back of a spoon. Season the sauce with salt and white pepper and set aside while preparing the garnish.

Place the butter for the garnish in a small frying pan and, when foaming, add the diced apples. Toss over a high heat until the apple is beginning to soften. Add a little sugar and cook until the sugar begins to caramelise.

To serve, coat the chicken with the sauce and garnish with watercress or parsley. Spoon the caramelised apples over the chicken.

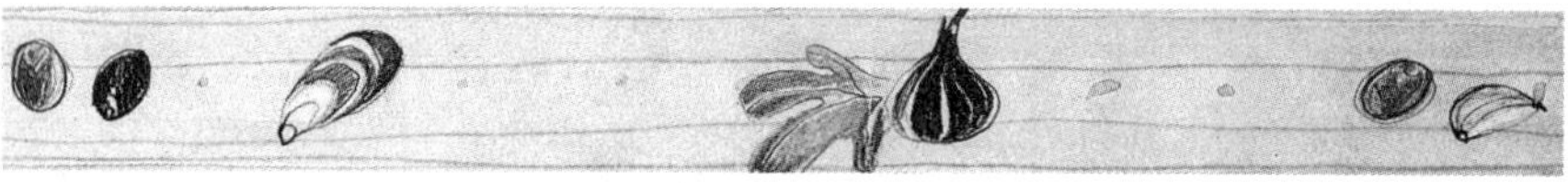

POULET AU RIZ
CHICKEN WITH RICE

This is a classic dish from the Alsace area of France. The chicken is flavoured with a variety of vegetables and then cream is added for a rich, smooth sauce. Cook the rice in your favourite way, but it is usually served boiled.

Serves 6

INGREDIENTS

1 large boiling chicken, cleaned and dried
Juice of 1 lemon
1 onion, chopped
1 carrot, chopped
1 leek, chopped
1 stick celery, finely chopped
1 bouquet garni
60g/2oz butter
60g/2oz flour
280ml/½ pint double cream
Salt and freshly ground black pepper
Cooked long-grain rice for serving

Put the chicken in a large saucepan and cover it with cold water. Bring to the boil and, as soon as the water is boiling well, remove the bird and drain well. Joint the chicken, separating the wings, thighs and the breasts. Sprinkle the lemon juice over the meat. Break up the carcass.

Put the carcass bones back into the saucepan, cover with fresh water, and add all the vegetables, the bouquet garni and the chicken portions. Bring to the boil, cover the pan, reduce the heat and simmer until the meat is tender. Remove the pieces of chicken and keep them warm. Boil what remains in the saucepan and allow it to reduce, skimming off any fat that rises to the top. Strain the sauce through a fine sieve and discard everything but the strained liquor.

Melt the butter in another saucepan and stir in the flour. Stir in the juices and continue stirring until the sauce boils and thickens. Cook for a few minutes more and then stir in the cream and add salt and pepper. Serve the pieces of chicken on a bed of boiled rice with the sauce poured over.

CHICKEN MARENGO

This was one of the first classic French dishes that I learnt when I was studying food at college! Created to celebrate Napoleons' victory at the Battle of Marengo, it reflects the ingredients that were available around the battle site, which was actually in Italy!

Serves 4

INGREDIENTS

60g/2oz butter
5 tbsps olive oil
1.4kg/3lbs chicken, jointed into 8 pieces
2 onions, finely sliced
1-2 plump cloves garlic, crushed
1 tbsp flour
400g/14oz can chopped tomatoes
430ml/¾ pint dark chicken stock
Salt and freshly ground black pepper
120g/4oz button mushrooms
1 truffle, sliced (optional)
Oil
4 small slices bread, crusts removed
4 eggs
Freshly chopped parsley to garnish

Heat the butter with 2 tbsps of the olive oil in a large frying pan or sauté pan, add the chicken pieces, a few at a time, and brown on all sides. Remove the chicken with a slotted spoon and set to one side.

Add the onions and garlic to the pan and cook slowly until softened. Increase the heat and brown the onions, then add the flour and cook for about 1 minute, until browned. Add the tomatoes and stock – 150ml/¼ pint of stock may be replaced with sherry if preferred. Bring the sauce to the boil, stirring constantly, then season to taste with salt and pepper.

Return the chicken to the pan and add the mushrooms and truffle, if used. Cover and simmer slowly for 1 hour, or until the chicken is tender.

Heat a little oil in a frying pan. Cut the bread into triangles and fry lightly until golden brown. Fry the eggs separately. Season the chicken, if necessary, transfer it to a serving dish and garnish with the fried bread and eggs. Sprinkle with chopped parsley and serve.

CHICKEN WITH TARRAGON SAUCE

Muscat de Beaumes de Venise gives a sweet richness of flavour to the popular marriage of poultry and tarragon. Ensure that the tarragon is French and not Russian – the former has a much finer flavour.

Serves 6

Ingredients

3 tbsps oil
120g/4oz butter
2 chickens, jointed
6 shallots, chopped
1 carrot, chopped
3 sprigs fresh tarragon
1 sherry glass Muscat de Beaumes de Venise
150ml/¼ pint white wine
280ml/½ pint chicken stock
Salt and freshly ground black pepper
1 tbsp cornflour mixed with 1 tbsp water (optional)
2 tbsps freshly chopped tarragon

Warm the oil and half the butter in a large flameproof casserole, add the chicken pieces and brown on all sides. Remove the chicken to a plate. Add the remaining butter to the casserole and cook the shallots, carrot and the sprigs of tarragon for 5 minutes. Slide the chicken pieces back into the casserole and stir well, then stir in the Muscat. Add the wine and the chicken stock, the salt and pepper, and stir well. Bring to the boil, cover, then reduce the heat and simmer for 30 minutes. Add a little water if necessary during cooking.

When the chicken pieces are cooked through, remove them and place in a preheated serving dish. Bring the sauce to the boil and allow it to reduce and thicken. If necessary, stir in the cornflour and water mixture, stirring continuously until the sauce has boiled and thickened. Season the sauce and serve it poured over the chicken. Sprinkle with the chopped tarragon.

CHICKEN ALSACE

This is a very rich recipe from Alsace. Use fine kitchen string to tie up the parcels of chicken if a caulfat is not available. Thicken the sauce if necessary with cornflour – I prefer not to if at all possible.

Serves 6

INGREDIENTS

1 large chicken, boned and cleaned (reserve the carcass, and liver)
1 egg, beaten
200ml/7fl oz double cream, whipped
Salt and freshly ground black pepper
2 tbsps Cognac
2 tbsps double cream
1 sheet of caulfat
75g/2½oz butter
1 carrot, shredded
1 leek (white part only), grated
1 onion, grated
150ml/¼ pint white wine
2 tbsps single cream
3 tbsps oil
60g/2oz raw foie gras (duck or goose liver)

Preheat the oven to 200°C/400°F/Gas Mark 6. Remove one of the chicken breasts and, in a liquidiser or food processor, blend it with the chicken liver, egg, whipped cream, salt and pepper. Rub this mixture through a fine sieve and add half the Cognac and the 2 tbsps of double cream to form a stiff paste. Spread this paste over the boned out chicken meat and then roll up neatly. Cut the meat into 6 pieces and cut the caulfat to fit around each piece of meat. If necessary, the ends can be secured by tying them up with fine kitchen string. Keep the chicken in a cool place.

Melt 60g/2oz of the butter in a heavy frying pan and cook the carrot, leek, onion and the broken up carcass for 5 minutes. Add the white wine and cover the bones with water. Bring to the boil and allow to cook until the sauce reduces a little and thickens slightly. Strain through a fine sieve and then put the sauce back in a saucepan over quite a high heat. Stir in the single cream and the remaining Cognac, and allow to reduce until quite thick.

Heat the remaining butter with the oil in a heavy frying pan and brown the pieces of meat on all sides. Roast in the hot oven for about 30 minutes. Just before serving, whisk the foie gras into the sauce, blending it with a hand mixer. Cut the meat into neat slices, remove any string, and pour the sauce over.

COQ AU VIN
CHICKEN IN RED WINE

This dish, under its French name of Coq au Vin, is one of the most famous chicken recipes in the world. It is hearty, rich and warming – a perfect cold weather classic and definitely not a dish for the summer!

Serves 4

Ingredients
225g/8oz thick cut streaky bacon
430ml/¾ pint water
12-16 button onions or shallots, quartered if large
30g/1oz butter
225g/8oz button mushrooms
1.4kg/3lb chicken, jointed into eight pieces
430ml/¾ pint dry red wine
3 tbsps brandy
1 bouquet garni
1 clove garlic, crushed
3 tbsps flour
430ml/¾ pint chicken stock
Salt and freshly ground black pepper
4 slices of bread, crusts removed
Oil for frying
2 tbsps freshly chopped parsley

Preheat the oven to 180°C/350°F/Gas Mark 4. Cut the bacon into strips about 6mm/¼ inch thick. Bring a pan of water to the boil and blanch the bacon by simmering it for 5 minutes in the water. Remove the bacon with a draining spoon and dry it on absorbent kitchen paper. Bring the water to the boil again and drop in the onions. Allow them to boil rapidly for 2-3 minutes and then plunge them into cold water and peel them. Set the onions aside with the bacon.

Melt half the butter in a large frying pan over a moderate heat and add the bacon and onions. Fry over a high heat, stirring frequently and shaking the pan, until the bacon and onions are golden brown. Remove them with a draining spoon and drain on absorbent kitchen paper. Add the remaining butter to the saucepan and cook the mushrooms for 1-2 minutes. Remove them and set them aside with the onions and bacon.

Reheat the frying pan and brown the chicken, a few pieces at a time. When all the pieces are browned, transfer the chicken to a large ovenproof casserole. Pour the wine into a small saucepan and boil it until reduced to about 280ml/½ pint. Pour the brandy into a small saucepan and warm it over a low heat. Ignite with a match and pour the brandy (while still flaming) over the chicken. Shake the casserole carefully until the flames die down. If the brandy should flare up, cover the casserole quickly with the lid. Add the bouquet garni and garlic to the casserole.

Pour off all but 1 tbsp of fat from the frying pan in which the vegetables were cooked, and stir in the flour. Cook over a gentle heat, scraping any of the browned chicken juices from the bottom of the pan. Pour in the reduced wine and add the stock. Bring the sauce to the boil over a high heat, stirring constantly until thickened. Strain over the chicken in the casserole and cover the dish tightly.

Place in the oven and cook for 20 minutes. Add the bacon, onions and mushrooms and continue cooking for a further 15-20 minutes, or until the chicken is tender. Remove the bouquet garni and season with salt and pepper.

Cut each slice of bread into 4 triangles. Heat enough oil in a large frying pan to cover the bread. When the oil is very hot, add the bread triangles, two at a time, and fry until golden brown and crisp. Drain on absorbent kitchen paper.

To serve, arrange the chicken in a deep dish, coat with the sauce and top with the vegetables, then arrange the fried bread around the outside of the dish. Sprinkle with freshly chopped parsley.

CHICKEN FRICASSÉE

This is a rich, creamy, classic white stew. It is thickened with a mixture of egg yolks and cream, a mixture which is called a liaison. Chicken fricassée is usually served with boiled rice and I would serve a tossed green salad after the chicken.

Serves 4

Ingredients
60g/2oz butter
1.4kg/3lb chicken, quartered and skinned
30g/1oz flour
570ml/1 pint chicken stock
Juice and grated rind of ½ a lemon
1 bouquet garni
12-16 small onions, peeled
340g/12oz small button mushrooms
2 egg yolks
90ml/3fl oz double cream
3 tbsps milk (optional)
Salt and white pepper
2 tbsps freshly chopped parsley and thyme, mixed
Lemon slices to garnish

Melt 45g/1½oz of the butter in a large sauté pan or frying pan. Add the chicken in one layer and cook over a gentle heat for about 5 minutes, or until the chicken is no longer pink. Do not allow the chicken to brown. Cook the chicken in two batches if necessary. When the chicken has lost its pinkness, remove it from the pan and set it to one side. Stir the flour into the butter remaining in the pan and cook over a very low heat, stirring continuously, for about 1 minute, or until a pale straw colour.

Remove the pan from the heat and gradually beat in the chicken stock. When blended smoothly, add the lemon juice and rind, return the pan to the heat and bring the sauce to the boil, whisking constantly. Reduce the heat and allow the sauce to simmer for 1 minute.

Return the chicken to the pan with any juices that have accumulated and add the bouquet garni. The sauce should almost cover the chicken. If it does not, add more stock or water. Bring to the boil, cover the pan and reduce the heat. Allow the chicken to simmer gently for 30 minutes.

Meanwhile, melt the remaining butter in a small frying pan, add the onions, cover and cook very gently for 10 minutes. Do not allow the onions to brown. Remove the onions from the pan with a draining spoon and add them to the chicken. Cook the mushrooms in the remaining butter for 2 minutes, then set them aside and add them to the chicken 10 minutes before the end of cooking.

Test the chicken by piercing a thigh portion with a sharp knife. It the juices run clear, the chicken is cooked. Transfer the chicken and vegetables to a serving dish and discard the bouquet garni. Skim the sauce of any fat and boil it rapidly to reduce by almost half.

Blend the egg yolks and cream together and whisk in several spoonfuls of the hot sauce. Return the egg yolk and cream mixture to the remaining sauce and cook gently for 2-3 minutes. Stir the sauce constantly and do not allow it to boil – you will get separated scrambled eggs! If it is very thick, add a little milk. Adjust the seasoning, stir in the parsley and thyme and spoon the sauce over the chicken in the serving dish. Garnish with lemon slices before serving.

TURKEY WITH FRESH TARRAGON

Turkey and tarragon go together very well – I often serve cold turkey in a tarragon mayonnaise. I would serve this creamy turkey dish with boiled rice.

Serves 6

Ingredients

3 large turkey breasts, about 900g-1kg/2-2¼lbs in total
Salt and freshly ground black pepper
2 tbsps oil
1 knob of butter
2 tbsps freshly chopped tarragon
2 tbsps port
280ml/½ pint chicken stock
1 tbsp cornflour, dissolved in 1 tbsp water
6 tbsps double cream

Preheat the oven to 190°C/375°F/Gas Mark 5. Sprinkle the turkey breasts with salt and pepper and then cook them in a flameproof casserole dish in the oil and butter until lightly browned. Pour off any excess fat, add the tarragon, port and stock, and stir well. Bring to the boil, then reduce the heat very slightly and allow to cook until the juices in the casserole have reduced by about a third. Cover the casserole dish and place in the preheated oven to finish cooking the turkey – this will take about 20 minutes. When the turkey is cooked through and ready to serve, remove the breasts and set aside. Stir the dissolved cornflour into the juices stirring continuously, and heat on the hob until the sauce thickens. Stir in the cream. Cut the breasts into thin slices and serve with the sauce poured over.

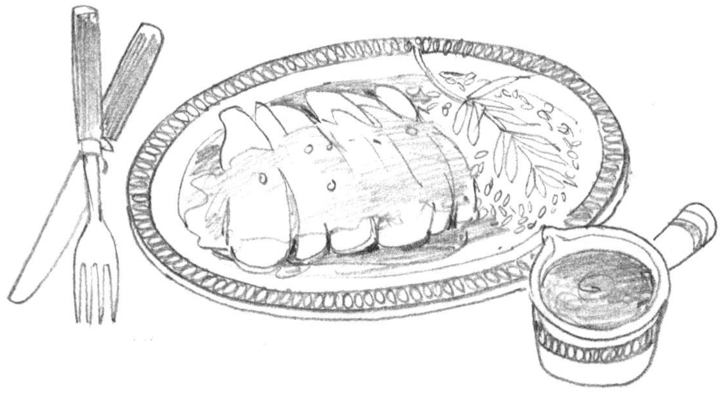

RABBIT IN MUSTARD SAUCE

Rabbit is popular in France, especially in traditional country dishes. It is light, lacking much of the heaviness of other dishes which are often flavoured and enriched with cream. Rabbit is often dressed with mustard – Dijon is still the home of the French mustard trade, producing around 50 per cent of the worlds' mustard.

Serves 4

INGREDIENTS

1.8kg/4lbs rabbit, cleaned and jointed
4 tbsps Dijon mustard
30g/1oz butter
1 tbsp oil
1 medium onion, finely chopped
30g/1oz plain flour
1 tbsp freshly chopped thyme
1 tsp fresh rosemary
430ml/¾ pint dry cider
Salt and freshly ground black pepper

Smear the rabbit pieces with the mustard and set aside for 2-3 hours to absorb the flavour. Heat the butter and oil together in a large frying pan and, when the foam subsides, fry the rabbit joints, a few at a time, until golden brown, then transfer them to a flameproof casserole dish.

Add the chopped onion to the frying pan, adding a little more oil if necessary. Fry the onion until soft and then add the flour and herbs, stirring constantly. Cook for 1-2 minutes over a gentle heat, then add the cider. Stir the sauce well and bring it to the boil. Season to taste, then pour the thickened sauce over the rabbit pieces. Cover the casserole and simmer gently for 45 minutes – 1 hour, until tender.

This dish is delicious served with buttered noodles and followed by a green salad. French bread could be served in place of the pasta, to mop up all the delicious juices.

LAPIN CHASSEUR
HUNTER'S RABBIT

Rabbit is an excellent country food to cook 'chasseur'– in the style of the hunter. Such dishes always include mushrooms, and sometimes bacon or tomatoes.

Serves 6

INGREDIENTS

1 rabbit, cleaned
120g/4oz smoked bacon, diced
1 onion, chopped
280ml/½ pint white wine
1 bouquet garni
Pinch of nutmeg
Salt and freshly ground black pepper
340g/¾lb mushrooms, sliced
1 tbsp butter
1 tbsp flour
1 tbsp freshly chopped parsley

Bone the rabbit and cut the meat into small pieces. Cook the bacon in a flameproof casserole on the hob, without adding any extra fat, until the fat from the bacon is running. Stir in the rabbit pieces, add the onion and continue cooking until the onion is soft. Pour in the wine and 280ml/½ pint water. Add the bouquet garni, nutmeg, and salt and pepper and bring to the boil. Cover the pan, reduce the heat and simmer for 30 minutes. Add the mushrooms and then simmer gently for a further 15 minutes.

Just before serving, beat together the butter and the flour. Gradually whisk this into the sauce, boiling the sauce between each addition, until the sauce thickens to the required consistency. Serve the rabbit with the parsley sprinkled over.

DUCK BREAST WITH GREEN PEPPERCORN SAUCE

Green peppercorns are often served with beef steaks either in a sauce or crushed over the meat. They make an unusual and delicious sauce for duck – spicy and rich.

Serves 6

Ingredients

1kg/2¼lbs duck or poultry bones and trimmings
1 tbsp oil
1 onion, finely chopped
1 carrot, finely chopped
1 leek, finely chopped
280ml/½ pint white wine
Salt and freshly ground black pepper
1 tsp thyme
1 bay leaf
3 large duck breasts
1 tbsp green peppercorns
1 tbsp Cognac
200ml/7fl oz double cream

Preheat the oven to 200°C/400°F/Gas Mark 6. Break up the bones and cook them in the oil in a heavy frying pan with the trimmings, 2 tbsps water, the onion, carrot and leek for 5 minutes. Add the white wine and enough water to cover. Add salt and pepper, the thyme and bay leaf, and bring to the boil. Allow to reduce by half. When the sauce has reduced, strain it through a fine sieve, then return it to the heat and reduce a little more.

Score the skin on the duck breasts and, in a clean frying pan, seal the breasts over a high heat, skin side first. Once sealed on all sides, continue cooking the duck in the preheated oven until just a thin line of pink is visible in the centre of the breasts – this takes about 10-15 minutes. Set the breasts aside and keep them warm.

Sauté the peppercorns in the fat from the duck breasts for 1 minute, add the Cognac, then stir in the reduced sauce. Allow this to reduce a little more and then stir in the cream. Season to taste. Cut the breasts into slices and serve with the sauce poured over.

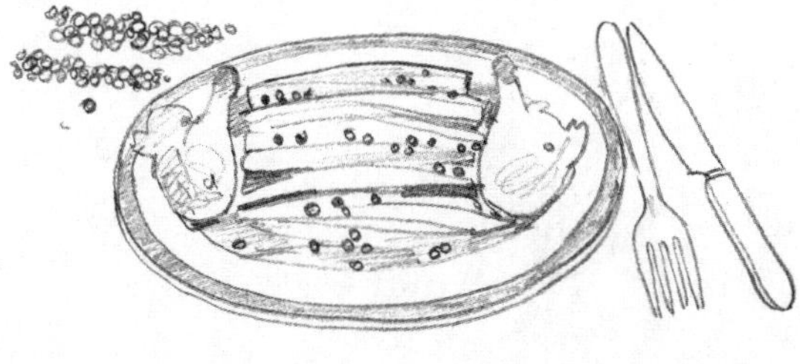

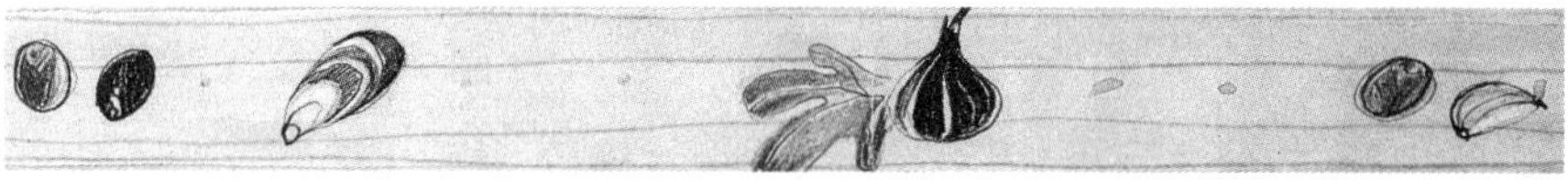

BRAISED DUCKLING WITH TURNIP SAUCE

This is a most unusual but delicious dish. Turnips are slightly peppery and complement the duckling well. I find that the best way to extract the juice from the turnips is to grate them, and then to squeeze the juice out in your clenched fist.

Serves 4-6

Ingredients
1 large duckling
1.4kg/3lbs turnips, peeled and sliced
3 onions, sliced
Juice of 3 large turnips
1 clove garlic
1 bouquet garni
Salt and freshly ground black pepper

Cut the duckling into pieces then brown them in a casserole without adding any more fat. Add the sliced turnips and continue cooking. Once the turnip has become slightly transparent, add 2 tbsps water, the onions, turnip juice, garlic, bouquet garni and salt and pepper. Cook over a very low heat for 20-30 minutes. Remove the bouquet garni, the duckling pieces and the turnip.

Blend the juices in a liquidiser or food processor until smooth. Add up to half of the cooked turnip, a little at a time, to thicken the sauce. Serve the duckling pieces interlaced with the remaining turnip slices, and pour the sauce around the edge of the dish.

DUCK À L'ORANGE
DUCK IN ORANGE SAUCE

Second only to Peking Duck, a classic Chinese dish, this must be one of the most famous recipes for duck in the world. I much prefer it to duck with black cherries – all too often jam is used in that sauce, making it far too sweet for my taste.

Serves 6

INGREDIENTS

8 oranges, washed and dried
75g/2½oz butter
1 large duck, prepared and cut into pieces
1 onion, finely chopped
1 carrot, scraped and shredded
1 tbsp vinegar
1 tbsp cornflour, dissolved in 1 tbsp water
Salt and freshly ground black pepper

Thinly peel 2 of the oranges with a potato peeler and cut the peel into fine strips. Blanch the strips in boiling water for a few minutes, drain well and set aside. Retain the oranges for their juice. Peel 4 more oranges removing all the white pith and cut the flesh into thick slices.

Melt two thirds of the butter in a heavy casserole and brown the duck pieces on all sides. Reduce the heat, add the onion, carrot and 2 tbsps of water. Cover and cook for about 30 minutes, turning the duck pieces from time to time. Add a little water if necessary during cooking. Remove the duck pieces from the casserole and wrap them tightly in aluminium foil to keep warm. Strain the juices from the casserole through a fine sieve into a clean saucepan. Squeeze the juice of the peeled oranges and the 2 remaining oranges, add this to the strained casserole juices and stir well. Add the vinegar and the orange strips. Cook over a low heat for a few minutes. Add the dissolved cornflour, stirring continuously, until the sauce boils and begins to thicken. Remove from the heat and season to taste. Cut the meat from the duck bones and place it on a serving dish. Cook the orange slices in the remaining butter in a small pan until they have taken on a little colour. Add them to the sauce, stir and serve the sauce poured over the duck.

QUAIL WITH GRAPES

Quail are becoming more and more popular, and many supermarkets now stock them 'oven-ready'. The grapes give a fragrance to the sauce, which should be served over or around the quail, sitting in splendour on freshly cooked croûtes or toasts.

Serves 6

INGREDIENTS
6 quail, cleaned and trussed
120g/4oz butter
2 tbsps oil
150ml/¼ pint Madeira
340g/¾lb seedless white grapes
570ml/1 pint rich chicken stock
Salt and freshly ground black pepper
6 slices of white bread

Preheat the oven to 200°C/400°F/Gas Mark 6. Heat a knob of the butter with 1 tbsp of the oil in a frying pan and gently brown the birds all over. Remove from the pan and finish cooking in the hot oven for about 15 minutes. Pour off any excess fat from the roasting tin and add the Madeira. Heat until almost evaporated, stirring up any meaty sediment from the bottom of the pan. Add the grapes and then stir in the stock. Allow to reduce to a syrupy consistency.

Remove the grapes using a slotted spoon. Stir in the remaining butter, reserving a knob for the toasts, and season the sauce with salt and pepper. Blend until smooth in a liquidiser or food processor then replace the grapes.

Fry the bread in the knob of butter with the remaining oil. Serve the quail on the toasts, with the sauce poured over.

PARTRIDGES WITH ARMAGNAC

This classic recipe combines many fine ingredients; partridges, cream, a truffle and Armagnac. It is luxurious, to be served on special occasions.

Serves 6

INGREDIENTS

3 young partridges, cleaned (retain the gizzards and the livers)
60g/2oz butter
1 tbsp olive oil
4 tbsps Armagnac
120ml/4fl oz double cream
1 truffle
Salt and freshly ground black pepper

Preheat the oven to 200°C/400°F/Gas Mark 6. Truss the birds with kitchen string. Heat one third of the butter with the oil in a heavy pan and brown the birds on all sides. Remove them from the saucepan (retain the juices) and finish cooking in the hot oven for 20 minutes.

Once the birds are cooked, cut off the wings, thighs and the breasts, set them aside and keep them warm.

Crush the carcasses and put them back into the saucepan containing the juices and add the gizzards and livers. Place over a high heat, add the Armagnac and the cream and stir well. Remove from the heat and strain through a fine sieve. Add the crumbled truffle and whisk in the remaining butter. Blend in a liquidiser or food processor until smooth, then season to taste.

Cut the partridges into slices and serve with the sauce poured over.

GUINEA FOWL CASSEROLE

Guinea fowl are very popular in the central regions of France.

Serves 6

Ingredients

225g/8oz smoked bacon, diced
1 onion, diced
3 carrots, diced
1 stick celery, diced
2 turnips, diced
2 large, young guinea fowl, cleaned, dried and cut into 4
2 tsps flour
150ml/¼ pint red wine
225g/8oz mushrooms, diced
2 tbsps double cream
Salt and freshly ground black pepper

Preheat the oven to 190°C/375°F/Gas Mark 5. Cook the bacon gently in a large flameproof casserole until the fat begins to run, then add the onion, carrots, celery and turnips. Cook until all the vegetables have turned slightly brown. Using a slotted spoon, remove all the above ingredients from the casserole to a plate. Add the guinea fowl pieces to the casserole, raise the heat and brown on all sides. Sprinkle with the flour, stir and cook for 1 minute. Add the wine, stirring continuously, then return all the ingredients from the plate. Stir in 200ml/7fl oz of water and add the mushrooms. Cover and cook in the oven until the fowl is cooked through, stirring from time to time – this will take about 30-40 minutes. Remove the guinea fowl, and the vegetables, then stir in the cream and drain the sauce through a fine sieve. Blend the sauce with a hand mixer or in a liquidiser. Season with a little salt and pepper. Serve the fowl on top of the blended sauce, covered with the mushroom and vegetable mixture.

PHEASANT WITH APPLES

This dish could hail from nowhere but Normandy – it contains pheasant, apples, calvados and cream. Don't be tempted to over-cook pheasant, which can easily become dry.

Serves 6

INGREDIENTS
60g/2oz butter
2 tbsps oil
2 thick rashers smoked bacon, diced
1 onion, finely chopped
1 large pheasant, wiped and cut into 6 pieces
5 cooking apples, peeled and sliced
3 tbsps Calvados
200ml/7fl oz double cream
Salt and freshly ground black pepper

Preheat the oven to 190°C/375°F/Gas Mark 5. Heat the butter with the oil in a large frying pan, add the bacon and onion and cook until soft. Remove with a slotted spoon and keep on a plate. Brown the pheasant pieces in the same frying pan. Remove to the plate once they are well coloured and sealed. Add the sliced apples to the same pan, season with salt and pepper and cook until browned. Add the cooked apple to the plate, then wipe out the frying pan with absorbent kitchen paper.

Put all the cooked ingredients back into the clean frying pan, add the Calvados and 150ml/¼ pint of water, cover and cook over a gentle heat for 10 minutes. Pour all the contents of the frying pan into a flameproof casserole, cover and finish cooking in the oven for 15 minutes. Stir in the cream halfway through cooking. Take the casserole out of the oven and remove the pheasant. Allow the sauce to reduce somewhat over a fairly high heat, then blend until smooth in a liquidiser or food processor. Put the sauce and pheasant pieces back into the casserole. Taste and adjust the seasoning if necessary, and serve immediately.

MEAT

The French really enjoy their food and meat is no exception. They pride themselves on their beef, they eat a lot of lamb, they still enjoy veal despite it being less fashionable now in so many other countries, and they eat a great deal of offal.

Charcuterie – a Great French Tradition

The French not only enjoy their meat roasted, casseroled and braised, they are also a nation of sausage lovers, enjoying countless varieties of *sauscisses sec*, the French answer to the salami of Italy and the smoked sausages of Germany.

The charcuterie centre of France is Lyon in Burgundy. The term Charcuterie (from *chair cuite* or cold meat) actually covers two groups of foods; prepared foods such as salads and baked pies, quiches etc; and any product of the pig. It is the latter group that is most commonly referred to as charcuterie. *Cervelas, Jesus salami, saucisson à l'ail* and the many hams cured in France are all rightfully placed amongst the best cold meat products in the world and the marvellous pâtés produced throughout France are certainly internationally acclaimed. Fresh hams take much of their flavour from the local grazing of the pigs – those fed on acorns in oak woods under the ancient right of *pannage* have the most wonderful flavour whilst, of the air-dried hams, the Jambon de Bayonne is probably my favourite.

A trip to the local market will reveal the local sausage specialities, many of which do not have recognisable names. I just choose one which the locals are buying, after tasting the readily proffered sample. I love the French sausage stands which are little more than a broom handle with the sausage draped over – I had one when I owned a delicatessen and it was a great selling feature; customers just decide how many centimetres of sausage they want and it is cut for them.

Most of the charcuterie products that I have described here are eaten cold, the preserved sausages sliced thinly and served with a glass of wine before a meal and many other products are simply served with toast or hot potatoes. Recipes for these foods don't exist – they are just to be enjoyed as they are. Why then, have I talked about them in such length in this introduction to French meat cookery? Well, charcuterie is so much a part of French life that it demands to be included in any description of meat in French cuisine.

Regional Pride

Although many dishes are regarded with fierce regional pride, careful examination will reveal that some of the dishes best known to those of us living outside France are simply regional variations on the same theme. For example, the local wine may change a beef stew from *Bourguignon* when cooked in Burgundy, to *Bordelais* when cooked in Bordeaux with the addition of marrow bone. I find the best wine for a *daube*, a beef stew from Provençe, is a Cotês du Rhône, again the local brew.

Vive La Difference!

Casseroles and stews are prepared in pretty much the same way the world over – the best are always cooked slowly with sympathetic seasoning to bring out the flavours in the meat. The French make time to cook their dishes slowly, showing real dedication and care in their preparation and cooking. You just cannot hurry something good!

French roasts are, however, cooked quite differently to the way in which traditional English roasts are cooked. First of all, the French are most particular that their meat should be well marbled with fat but they trim most of the fat surrounding a joint away. Lamb cutlets with the fat cut away from the bones right down to the eye of the meat are referred to as '*French trimmed*' or '*Frenched*', and this method of preparation is also applied to joints for roasting. The meat is also cooked very quickly at a very high temperature (usually 220°C/425°F/Gas Mark 7), producing a well cooked outside and a very pink, rare centre. This is exactly how the French like their meat, but it is not to everyone's taste – most medium to well-cooked meats need longer cooking at a more moderate temperature. This high temperature roasting produces a great deal of splatter in the oven, which is why more ovens with catalytic cleaning (a high temperature method of burning any spatter off the oven walls) are sold in France than in any other country in Europe!

PORK FILLET WITH PRUNES

An easy meal to prepare and cook, with a delicious, slightly sweet sauce.

Serves 6

INGREDIENTS

1kg/2¼lbs pork fillet
20 rashers smoked bacon
1 tbsp olive oil
1 shallot, finely chopped
½ carrot, finely chopped
2 tbsps port
280ml/½ pint chicken stock
225g/8oz pitted prunes
Salt and freshly ground black pepper

Preheat the oven to 180°C/350°F/Gas Mark 4. Remove any fat or gristle from the meat. Cut the meat into medallions, roll a strip of bacon around the sides of each medallion and secure with kitchen string. Heat the olive oil in a frying pan and seal the medallions on all sides. Place the medallions in a roasting tin in the preheated oven and cook for about 20 minutes. Cooking time will depend on the thickness of the meat and individual taste.

Remove any excess oil from the frying pan, leaving about 1 tablespoon, and gently cook the shallot and carrot. Increase the heat, add the port and then the stock. Bring to the boil and allow to reduce by about a third. Pour the sauce into a liquidiser or food processor and blend, adding three quarters of the pitted prunes, a few at a time, until the mixture is smooth. Return the sauce to the heat, season to taste, and warm through. Serve the medallions on the sauce, and decorate with the remaining whole prunes.

PETIT SALÉ AUX LENTILLES
HAM WITH LENTILS

This is a real country dish. The French name 'petit salé' actually means small and salty. Be careful with the seasoning – remember the ham will be quite salty. I sometimes add a few spoonfuls of mustard to this dish.

Serves 6

INGREDIENTS
1.15kg/2½lbs boneless ham
6 small herb sausages
900g/2lbs green lentils
1 large onion, stuck with 2 whole cloves
225g/8oz carrots, cut into chunks
1 bouquet garni
Salt and freshly ground black pepper

Wash the ham under running water, then place it in a large saucepan and cover with cold water. Bring to the boil, reduce the heat and simmer for 2 hours. After 2 hours, add the sausages to the saucepan, cook for a further 10 minutes and then remove the pan from the heat.

Cook the lentils in a large quantity of water with the onion, carrot, bouquet garni and a little salt. Bring them gently to the boil, reduce the heat and simmer for 30-40 minutes. Do not boil too rapidly or the lentils will disintegrate. After about 30 minutes, add the ham and the sausages and continue cooking until the lentils are tender. Drain off a little liquid, if necessary, and remove the bouquet garni. Cut the meat and the sausages into chunks, put back into the saucepan, heat through again and serve.

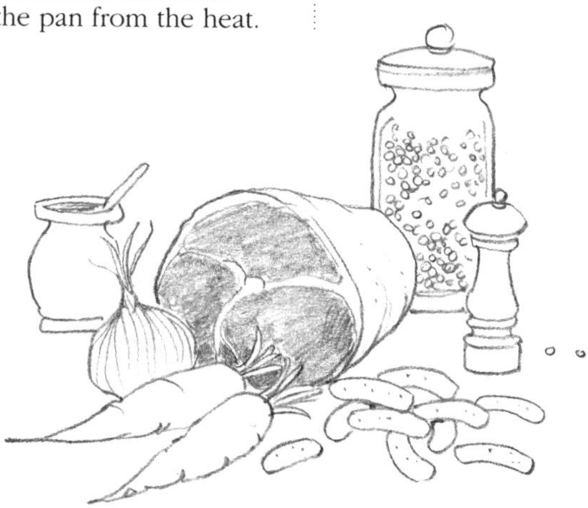

ROAST PORK WITH GARLIC CREAM

This creamy sauce, well flavoured with garlic, makes a marvellous accompaniment to lean roast pork. Brown the pork well before transferring it to the oven to finish cooking.

Serves 6

INGREDIENTS

1kg/2¼lbs boneless loin of pork
2 tbsps olive oil
1 whole head garlic, all the cloves peeled
100ml/3½fl oz port
280ml/½ pint double cream, whipped
Salt and freshly ground black pepper
Knob of butter

Preheat the oven to 200°C/400°F/Gas Mark 6. Trim any excess fat or gristle from the meat, setting the trimmings aside for use in the sauce, then roll the meat into a roast and secure it with string. Sauté the meat trimmings in half the oil with the garlic, and allow to brown slightly. Pour off any excess fat from the pan and stir in the port. Remove from the heat and stir in the cream. Remove a few cloves of garlic for decoration. Blend the sauce until smooth in a liquidiser and then strain it through a fine sieve into a clean pan. Return the sauce to the heat and allow it to reduce a little. Remove from the heat.

Heat the remaining oil and the butter in a large frying pan and seal the pork on all sides. Transfer it to a roasting tin and cook in the preheated oven for 20-40 minutes, depending on the thickness of the roast. Reheat the sauce gently. Slice the pork and serve with the sauce poured over and the few cloves of garlic as garnish.

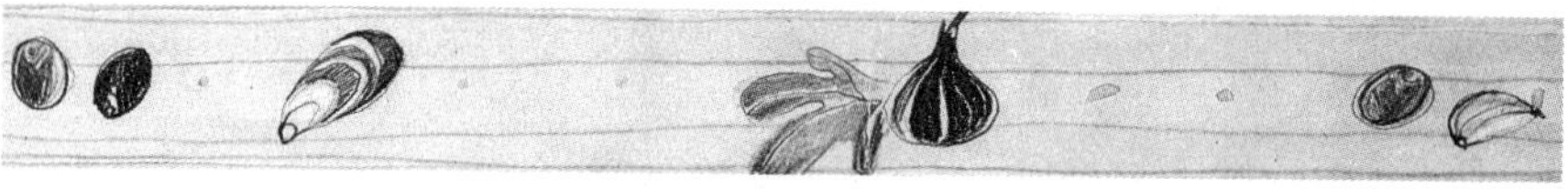

PORK PROVENÇALE

I always feel that there aren't sufficient casserole recipes for pork – but, of course, the French have plenty! The pork is flavoured with tomatoes and herbs and topped with sliced potatoes.

Serves 6

INGREDIENTS

1kg/2¼lbs pork fillets or tenderloins
60g/2oz butter
340g/¾lb onions, thinly sliced
400g/14oz can tomatoes
Salt and freshly ground black pepper
1 tbsp freshly chopped mixed herbs
680g/1½lb potatoes, thinly sliced
1 tbsp freshly chopped parsley

Preheat the oven to 180°C/350°F/Gas Mark 4. Trim the pork of any surplus fat and slice it thinly. Melt half the butter in a large sauté pan and gently fry the slices of meat, stirring continuously to prevent them from burning. Transfer the meat to a plate and set aside. Stir the onions into the meat juices in the sauté pan and cook gently until just soft. Add the tomatoes to the pan along with the salt, pepper and mixed herbs. Bring to the boil, then simmer gently for 5 minutes, or until the sauce has reduced by about a third.

Arrange the meat, sauce and potatoes in layers in an ovenproof serving dish, finishing with a layer of potato. Melt the remaining butter and brush it over the top layer of potato. Cover the dish with a lid or foil, and cook in the preheated oven for 1½ hours. Remove the lid from the dish and continue cooking for a further 30 minutes to brown the potatoes. Sprinkle with chopped parsley before serving.

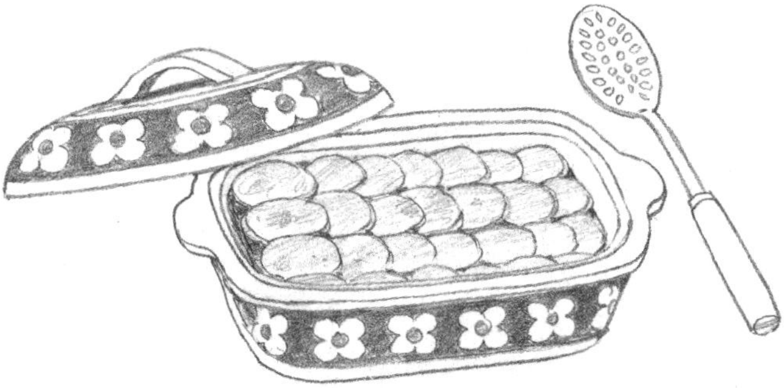

CASSOULET

Cassoulet has almost as many recipes as I've had hot dinners! The main ingredient is haricot beans and it should include a mixture of meats. I often place a layer of breadcrumbs over my cassoulet and brown them, uncovered, in the oven.

Serves 6–8

INGREDIENTS

460g/1lb haricot beans, presoaked for 12 hours
60g/2oz goose or other poultry dripping
1 pork knuckle
460g/1lb pork loin
1 onion, sliced
2 cloves garlic, chopped
1 leek, cut into chunks
4 tomatoes, halved
1 carrot, cut into chunks
1 bay leaf
1 bouquet garni
225g/8oz herb or garlic sausages
340g/¾lb bacon, in one piece
½ shoulder lamb
Salt and freshly ground black pepper

Drain and rinse the haricot beans. Melt the dripping in a large flameproof casserole and fry the pork knuckle and the loin to seal. Then add the onion, garlic, leek, tomatoes, carrot, bay leaf and the bouquet garni. Stir well and cook for a few minutes. Add the drained beans, and enough water to cover the contents of the casserole. Bring to the boil then reduce the heat, cover and simmer slowly for 2 hours. After about one hour, add the sausages, bacon, and the shoulder of lamb. Check the water level during cooking and add water when necessary. After the full 2 hours, strain off the juice into a clean saucepan and chop the meat into bite–sized pieces. Discard most of the bones. Remove the bay leaf and the bouquet garni.

Preheat the oven to 190°C/375°F/Gas Mark 5. In a large earthenware bowl, places layers of the chopped meats, beans and sausages. Add 570–850/1–1½ pints of the cooking liquor, cover and continue cooking in the hot oven for 35 minutes. Serve piping hot from the oven.

SAUTÉ D'AGNEAU
LAMB IN RED WINE

This is a quick and easy recipe to cook. The rich mushroom sauce is very special. I like to serve this with buttered noodles.

Serves 4

Ingredients
2 tbsps olive oil
1kg/2¼lbs shoulder of lamb, boned and cubed
3 sticks celery, sliced
1 onion, finely chopped
225g/8oz mushrooms
175ml/6fl oz red wine
175ml/6fl oz beef stock
1 tbsp tomato purée
2 tbsps cornflour mixed with 2 tbsps water
Salt and freshly ground black pepper

Warm half the olive oil in a frying pan and seal the pieces of lamb on all sides. Allow to brown slightly, then remove the lamb from the pan with a draining spoon and keep it warm. Add the remaining oil and sauté the celery, onion and mushrooms until softened. Add the wine, stock, tomato purée and the dissolved cornflour. Stir until the sauce boils and thickens, heating gently. Return the lamb to the frying pan with the sauce, add a little salt and pepper, cover and cook for a further 15-25 minutes. Remove the lamb and purée the sauce in a blender until smooth. Serve the meat with the sauce poured over.

FILLET OF LAMB WITH FRESH THYME SAUCE

Lamb is very popular in France. Especially at the start of the season it is cooked very pink in the centre – you may need to roast the lamb for about 45 minutes if you prefer it well done. This recipe is a celebration of spring lamb.

Serves 6

Ingredients

120ml/4fl oz olive oil
1 saddle of lamb, boned but kept whole (reserve bones for the sauce)
1 carrot, finely chopped
1 onion, finely chopped
120ml/4fl oz dry white wine
4 sprigs fresh thyme
150g/5oz butter
Salt and freshly ground black pepper

Preheat the oven to 200°C/400°F/Gas Mark 6. Heat half the olive oil in a large pan and sauté the lamb bones with the carrot and onion. Drain off any excess fat, then add the wine and heat until almost evaporated, stirring continuously. Cover the ingredients with water and cook at a gentle boil, uncovered, for 1 hour. Strain the juices through a very fine sieve into a clean saucepan. Cook over a high heat, with the thyme, and allow to reduce until quite thick.

Heat 30g/1oz of the butter and the remaining oil in the frying pan and seal the lamb on all sides. Transfer it to a roasting tin and finish cooking the lamb in the hot oven for 15 minutes. Just before serving, strain the reduced juices through a fine sieve to remove the thyme. Mix the remaining butter into the sauce, a little at a time, and blend until smooth with a hand mixer or whisk. Cut the lamb into slices and serve with the sauce.

FILET D'AGNEAU EN CROÛTE
FILLET OF LAMB IN PASTRY

'En croute' means wrapped in pastry. Fillet of beef is often cooked in this way and is a real treat – fillet of lamb is also delicious and much more affordable!

Serves 6

INGREDIENTS
2 lamb fillets, cut from the neck or the loin
Salt and freshly ground black pepper
1 tbsp olive oil
90g/3oz butter
1 carrot, finely chopped
1 onion, finely chopped
1 sprig thyme
1 bay leaf
280ml/½ pint white wine
225g/8oz prepared puff pastry
1 clove garlic, chopped
2 tbsps freshly chopped parsley
1 egg, beaten

Preheat the oven to 220°C/425°F/Gas Mark 7. Prepare the lamb fillets, removing and retaining any fat or gristle for the sauce. Lightly pepper the meat. Warm the oil and a knob of butter in a frying pan, and seal the meat on all sides. Remove the meat with a slotted spoon and keep warm. Sauté the lamb trimmings, carrot, onion, thyme, and the bay leaf in the pan. Wipe out the excess fat and add the white wine to the pan. Boil until almost evaporated, scraping up any meat sediment. Cover the vegetables with water, bring to the boil then skim off any fat which rises to the surface, and to reduce and thicken.

Roll out the pastry very thinly and cut into 2 rectangles. Place the fillets on to the pastry, sprinkle with the chopped garlic and parsley, and fold the pastry round the fillets. Seal the edges with the beaten egg, and brush a little egg over the top. Cook in the hot oven for about 15 minutes, until the pastry is browned and crisp. Strain the thickened sauce through a fine sieve, return it to the heat in a clean saucepan and allow it to reduce a little and thicken. Stir in the remaining butter. Cut the encased fillet into slices and serve with the sauce.

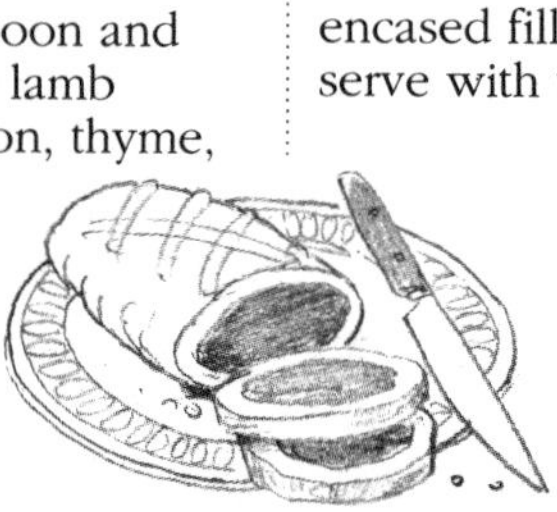

LAMB PROVENÇALE

Use red or white wine in this Mediterranean-style lamb casserole. I actually think that white wine produces a better flavour for lamb when it is cooked in this way, but make sure that you use a dry white wine.

Serves 4

INGREDIENTS
460g/1lb lamb from a cooked leg
60g/2oz butter
1 tbsp olive oil
2 medium onions, chopped
1 clove garlic, crushed
400g/14oz can tomatoes
1 tbsp tomato purée
280ml/½ pint dry white wine
120g/4oz mushrooms, sliced
1 large green pepper, seeded and sliced
Salt and freshly ground black pepper

Cut the lamb into small dice. Heat the butter with the olive oil, add the onions and garlic and cook gently for 10-15 minutes until softened but not browned. Stir in the tomatoes, tomato purée and wine and bring to the boil. Add the lamb, cover the pan and simmer for 25 minutes. Add the prepared mushrooms and green pepper and cook for a further 15 minutes, stirring occasionally. Season to taste and serve.

NAVARIN PRINTANIER
LAMB WITH SPRING VEGETABLES

This stew is traditionally made with mutton, such dishes are now usually made with lamb.

Serves 6

INGREDIENTS
90ml/3fl oz vegetable oil
12 evenly sized lamb cutlets
Flour mixed with salt, pepper and pinch of dried thyme
2 shallots, finely chopped
1 clove garlic, crushed
570ml/1 pint brown stock
150ml/¼ pint dry white wine
5 tomatoes, skinned, seeded and roughly chopped
1 bouquet garni

Spring Vegetables
12 new potatoes, scrubbed but not peeled
8 baby carrots, scraped (if green tops are in good condition, leave them on)
6 small turnips, peeled and left whole
225g/8oz French beans, cut into 2.5cm/1 inch lengths on the diagonal
340g/¾lb frozen petits pois
12 spring onions, roots ends and green tops trimmed, about 7.5cm/3 inches in length
1 tbsp freshly chopped parsley (optional)

Preheat the oven to 180°C/350°F/Gas Mark 4. Heat about half the oil in a large, heavy-based frying pan. Dredge the lamb cutlets with the flour mixture, shaking off any excess. Brown the cutlets 4 at a time, adding more oil if necessary. When the cutlets are brown on all sides, transfer them to a heavy flameproof casserole. Drain most of the oil from the pan, add the shallots and garlic and cook over a moderate heat, stirring constantly. Add the stock and wine and bring to the boil, scraping the bottom of the pan to remove the browned meat juices. Allow to boil rapidly to reduce slightly, then add the tomatoes. Pour the sauce over the lamb, turning the cutlets to coat them with the sauce. Add the bouquet garni, cover the casserole tightly and cook in the oven for about 30 minutes, or until the lamb is tender.

After about 10 minutes, add the potatoes and carrots to the lamb. Add the turnips, French beans, peas and spring onions 15 minutes before the end of the cooking time. After 30 minutes, remove the lamb and any vegetables that are tender to a warmed serving dish. Boil the sauce rapidly to reduce it and to cook any vegetables that need extra time. Pour the sauce over the lamb and vegetables and sprinkle with chopped parsley, if wished.

BEEF BOURGUIGNON

A classic dish from Burgundy, so choose a good red wine of that region for cooking. A long slow cook and prime ingredients are the real secrets of success!

Serves 6-8

INGREDIENTS

6 rashers smoked streaky bacon, cut into small pieces
20 baby onions, peeled
1 tbsp olive oil
2kg/4½lbs braising steak, cut into cubes
2 tbsps flour
1 bottle red wine
Salt and freshly ground black pepper

In a large saucepan cook the bacon and the onions without adding any extra fat. Remove them with a slotted spoon once they begin to brown. Add the oil and the meat and cook quickly to brown and seal the meat on all sides. Sprinkle with the flour and allow it to brown slightly, then add the wine, stirring well. Add water to cover only if necessary. Add salt and pepper and bring to the boil. Reduce the heat and return the onions and bacon to the pan. Cover and simmer very slowly for 3 hours, or until the beef is tender. Season and serve hot.

TOURNEDOS MAÎTRE D'HÔTEL
TOURNEDOS STEAKS WITH HERB BUTTER

Tournedos steaks are cut from the very best end of the fillet. They are a real treat and should, I think, be cooked simply. In this recipe they are served with a herb butter – 'maître d'hôtel.'

Serves 6

INGREDIENTS

120g/4oz butter, softened at room temperature
2 tbsps freshly chopped herbs
1 tsp lemon juice
Salt and freshly ground black pepper
6 tournedos steaks

Beat the butter in a bowl until quite soft. Add the herbs and beat well, then add the lemon juice and a little salt and pepper. Place the butter on a sheet of aluminium foil and form it into a roll. Place the butter in the freezer to harden.

Cook the steaks under a hot grill to your own preference and serve on a warmed dish topped with the cold butter cut into slices – one slice on each steak.

HUNTER'S TOURNEDOS STEAKS

This rich mushroom sauce, a classic used in many French dishes, may be served over any steaks, chicken portions or pork fillet. Use white wine if you prefer, but I like red best!

Serves 6

INGREDIENTS
60g/2oz butter
225g/8oz mushrooms, sliced
1 tbsp freshly chopped tarragon
60g/2oz shallots, chopped
3 tbsps Cognac
120ml/4fl oz red wine
225ml/8fl oz beef stock
Salt and freshly ground black pepper
6 tournedos steaks

Melt one third of the butter in a frying pan and cook the mushrooms, tarragon and shallots until tender. Add the Cognac and cook until almost evaporated. Stir in the wine and the stock and season well. Allow the sauce to reduce until quite thick and syrupy.

Cook the steaks to your liking under a hot grill. Whisk the remaining butter into the sauce and serve it poured over the steaks.

BLANQUETTE DE VEAU WHITE VEAL STEW

A white stew is known as a 'blanquette', and is usually made with white meat – veal, pork or chicken. Chicken is the best alternative to veal for this recipe. Garnish with chopped parsley or watercress.

Serves 4

INGREDIENTS
460g/1lb boneless veal, diced
2 onions, chopped
1 leek, chopped
2 carrots, chopped
Salt and white pepper
30g/1oz butter
2 tbsps plain flour
175g/6oz button mushrooms, sliced
1 egg yolk, beaten
200ml/7fl oz milk
200ml/7fl oz single cream

Place the cubes of meat in a large flameproof casserole, cover with cold water and bring to the boil. Add the onions, leek, carrots and salt and pepper. Return to the boil, then reduce the heat and cover the casserole. Cook until the meat is tender, skimming off the fat that rises to the surface from time to time – this will take about 1 hour. Remove the cooked meat with a slotted spoon, and keep it warm.

Melt the butter and stir in the flour. Gradually add the cooking liquor from the casserole, stirring continuously, and heat until the sauce boils and thickens. Add the mushrooms, reduce the heat and cook for 15 minutes, stirring regularly. Beat the milk and the cream into the egg yolk, and beat half of this mixture into the sauce. Once it is well incorporated, beat in the remaining mixture, beating continuously to avoid curdling. Do not allow the sauce to boil. Add the sauce to the meat, heat through and serve in a preheated serving dish.

SIRLOIN STEAK WITH CIDER SAUCE

A dish from Normandy featuring apples and cider but, surprisingly, no cream! Carve the steak into slices at the table if you prefer – it looks impressive!

Serves 4

Ingredients
75g/2½oz butter
2 tbsps oil
1 shallot, chopped
1 apple, peeled, cored and sliced
570ml/1 pint dry cider
280ml/½ pint beef stock
1 piece sirloin steak, weighing about 1kg/2¼lbs

Heat 15g/½oz of butter in a frying pan with the oil, add the shallot and the apple slices and cook until tender. Add the cider, increase the heat and allow the juices to reduce. Stir in the stock and allow the sauce to reduce once again – but not too much as the apples will make the sauce quite thick. Push the contents of the pan through a fine sieve then blend in a liquidiser or food processor until smooth.

Cook the steak to your liking in a frying pan, then carve it into slices. Arrange on a preheated serving dish. Reheat the sauce and whisk in the remaining butter before serving.

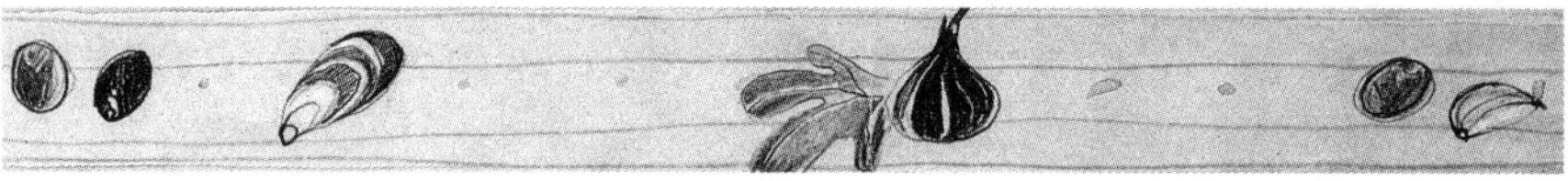

STEAK AU POIVRE
STEAK IN GREEN PEPPERCORN SAUCE

Green peppercorns are pretty hot, so reduce the quantity used in this recipe if you are cautious by nature!

Serves 4

INGREDIENTS
90g/3oz green peppercorns in brine
2 tbsps Dijon mustard
4 fillet steaks
45g/1½oz butter
225ml/8fl oz double cream
½ tsp salt
1 tbsp freshly chopped parsley

Drain the peppercorns and rinse them. Pat dry on absorbent kitchen paper and crush them in a pestle and mortar or in a small bowl, using the end of a rolling pin. Mix the crushed peppercorns with the mustard and spread this on both sides of the steaks. Melt the butter in a large, heavy-based frying pan over a high heat. When the foam subsides, add the steaks and fry for 2 minutes on each side. This will produce rare steaks. Double the time for medium–rare and allow about 12 minutes for well-done steaks. Remove the steaks from the pan to a serving dish and keep them warm while you finish the sauce.

Add the cream and salt to the pan and cook gently for a few minutes, scraping all the sediment from the bottom of the pan and incorporating it into the sauce.

Remove the pan from the heat and pour the sauce over the steaks. Sprinkle with parsley and serve at once.

CARBONNADE À LA FLAMANDE
BEEF IN BEER

Cooking beef in beer gives a dish known as a 'Carbonnade'. These are more common in the north of France, towards the Flemish border, where more 'dark beer', brown ale or bitter, is drunk. I sometimes spoon a little crème fraîche into a Carbonnade before serving.

Serves 6

INGREDIENTS
2 tbsps oil
680g/1½lb braising steak
1 large onion, thinly sliced
30g/1oz flour
1 clove garlic, crushed
280ml/½ pint brown ale
280ml/½ pint hot water
Bouquet garni
Salt and freshly ground black pepper
Pinch of sugar
Nutmeg
Dash of red wine vinegar
6 slices French bread cut about 1.25cm/½ inch thick
Dijon mustard

Preheat the oven to 160°C/325°F/Gas Mark 3. Heat the oil in a large, heavy-based frying pan. Cut the meat into 5cm/2 inch pieces and brown quickly on both sides in the oil. Brown the meat 5-6 pieces at a time to avoid crowding the pan.

Remove the meat from the pan to a casserole when browned, lower the heat and add the onion to the pan. Cook until the onion is beginning to soften and colour, then stir in the flour and add the garlic. Cook for about 1 minute. Add the ale and hot water, the bouquet garni, salt and pepper, and add a little sugar, nutmeg and vinegar. Bring to the boil then transfer to the casserole with the meat, cover and cook in the oven for 2-2½ hours.

Fifteen minutes before serving, skim off any fat from the surface and reserve it. Spread the mustard on the bread and spoon some of the fat over each slice.

Place the bread on top of the casserole, pushing it down slightly. Cook a further 15-20 minutes, uncovered, or until the bread is browned and crisp.

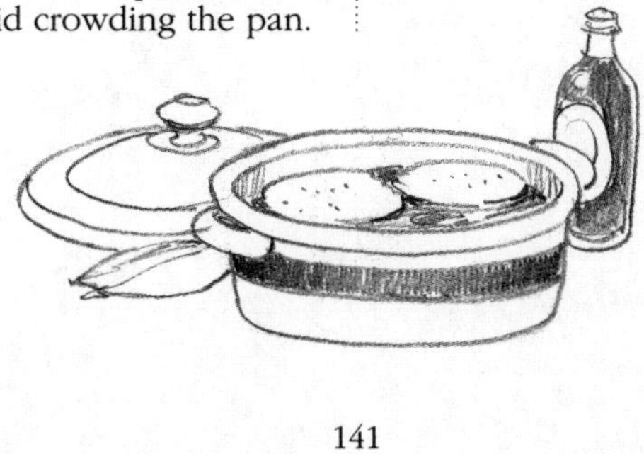

BOEUF EN DAUBE

As with so many classic dishes, there are countless recipes for daube – a rich beef stew originally cooked in a daubière, an earthenware cooking pot. I often add a little orange rind and lots of thyme to the basic recipe.

Serves 6

Ingredients
1kg/2¼lbs chuck steak
225g/8oz smoked bacon, diced
4 sprigs parsley
4 cloves garlic, chopped
Salt and freshly ground black pepper
2 tbsps olive oil
2 onions, chopped
2 carrots, chopped
1 bottle red wine

Remove any excess fat from the meat and cut into quite large cubes. Slice the cubes open on one side and place a little bacon, parsley, garlic, salt and pepper in each. Close each cube of meat and secure with a cocktail stick. Warm the olive oil in a frying pan and seal the meat on all sides. Remove the cocktail sticks. Empty the contents of the pan into a flameproof casserole, add the onion, carrot, and the wine. Bring to the boil and allow the liquid to reduce a little. Cover and continue cooking over a gentle heat for 3 hours. Check the level of the juices from time to time, stir, and add water if necessary. Season to taste and serve.

ESTOUFFADE DE BOEUF
BEEF WITH OLIVES

A rich beef casserole, similar to a daube, but with the flavourings of Provençe – olives, thyme and mushrooms. This is one of my favourite dishes!

Serves 6

INGREDIENTS
2 tbsps olive oil
225g/8oz smoked bacon, diced
1kg/2¼lbs best braising steak, cut into bite-sized pieces
2 tbsps plain flour
4 onions, sliced
Salt and freshly ground black pepper
1 bottle dry red wine
1 bouquet garni (with lots of thyme)
2 cloves garlic, chopped
175g/6oz mushrooms, sliced
120g/4oz pitted black olives

Preheat the oven to 160°C/325°F/Gas Mark 3. Heat 1 tbsp of the olive oil in a large, flameproof casserole and cook the bacon until the juices run. Toss the beef in the flour and shake off any excess. Add to the casserole with the bacon and the onions and brown the meat on all sides. Drain off any excess fat. Add salt and pepper and the wine. Stir well, then allow the wine to reduce over a high heat, until about half of the liquid remains. Add the bouquet garni and the garlic, cover and cook in the preheated oven for 2 hours, checking and stirring from time to time.

Sauté the mushrooms in the remaining olive oil. Strain the contents of the casserole through a large sieve, catching the juices in a clean saucepan. Place the meat and onions back in the casserole dish and add the sautéed mushrooms. Return the juices to the heat, skim off any rising fat, then stir in the olives. Pour this sauce back over the contents of the casserole and cook in the oven or on the hob for a further 20 minutes. Remove the bouquet garni and season to taste. Serve hot.

NORMANDY VEAL WITH APPLES AND CALVADOS

Most supermarkets now sell turkey escalopes, which could be used in place of veal in this traditional dish from Normandy. Do not overcook the meat – it needs a very short cooking time.

Serves 4

INGREDIENTS

2 dessert apples
120g/4oz butter
60g/2oz mushrooms, thinly sliced
4 120g/4oz veal escalopes, beaten thin
Salt and freshly ground black pepper
4 tbsps Calvados
150ml/¼ pint double cream or thick yogurt
2 tbsps lemon juice
1 tbsp freshly chopped chives or parsley

Peel, core and thinly slice the apples. Melt the butter in a large frying pan and, when it starts to foam, add the apple and mushroom slices and sauté gently until tender and just starting to brown. Remove the apples and mushrooms and set aside. Season the escalopes with salt and pepper, add to the pan and fry quickly on both sides.

Warm the Calvados in a small saucepan, set it alight and pour it over the veal. Gently move the frying pan so the liqueur is evenly distributed, until the flames die down. Reduce the heat and add the cream or yogurt, the lemon juice and the apples and mushrooms. Cook for a further 2-3 minutes, stirring continuously until the sauce starts to thicken. Do not boil. Transfer the escalopes to a hot serving dish, adjust the seasoning of the sauce if necessary and pour the sauce over the meat. Garnish with the chives or parsley.

ROGNONS À LA DIJONNAISE
KIDNEYS WITH DIJON MUSTARD

This is my favourite way of serving kidneys! Use a smooth Dijon mustard for this smooth, rich sauce. I serve the kidneys with rice or pasta, and then follow it up with a tossed green salad.

Serves 6

INGREDIENTS
680g/1½lb lambs' kidneys
60g/2oz unsalted butter
1-2 shallots, finely chopped
280ml/½ pint dry white wine
90g/3oz lightly salted butter, softened
3 tbsps Dijon mustard
Salt, freshly ground black pepper and lemon juice, to taste
2 tbsps freshly chopped parsley

Trim away any fat from the kidneys and slice them in half lengthways. Carefully snip out any hard core from the centre using a pair of sharp scissors. Melt the unsalted butter in a large frying pan and gently sauté the kidneys, uncovered, until they are lightly browned on all sides. Remove the kidneys from the frying pan with a slotted spoon and keep them warm. Add the shallots to the meat juices in the pan and cook for about 1 minute, stirring frequently, until they are just soft. Add the wine and bring to the boil, stirring constantly and scraping the bottom of the pan to remove any browned juices. Boil the sauce rapidly for 3-4 minutes to reduce it by about half. Remove the pan from the heat. Add the softened butter to the pan with the mustard and seasonings. Whisk the mixture into the reduced sauce with a small whisk or fork. Return the pan to the heat and add the kidneys and the parsley. Heat very gently for 1-2 minutes, taking care not to boil the mixture any further. Serve immediately.

KIDNEYS TURBIGO

Always use freshly ground black pepper in this dish to achieve a spicy flavour. The sauce is rich and the dish needs little more than creamy mashed potatoes served with it.

Serves 4-6

INGREDIENTS
8 lambs' kidneys
6 chipolata sausages
12 button onions
60g/2oz butter
30g/1oz plain flour
430ml/¾ pint stock – beef or chicken
150ml/¼ pint dry white wine
2 tsps tomato purée
3 tbsps dry or medium dry sherry
Salt and freshly ground black pepper
1 bay leaf
Parsley and croûtons to garnish

Cut the kidneys in half, removing the white core and any skin, and also cut the sausages. Melt the butter in a large, heavy-based pan and fry the kidneys and sausages until they are well browned. Remove from the pan and keep hot.

Peel the button onions, leaving them whole and place them in a pan of cold water. Bring to the boil and allow to simmer for 5 minutes, then drain.

Return to the pan containing the butter and meat juices, stir in the flour and cook for 2-3 minutes. Gradually add the stock and wine, stirring the whole time until the sauce is thickened and smooth. Bring to the boil and blend in the tomato purée and sherry. Season to taste. Return the kidneys and sausages to the pan, together with the drained onions and the bay leaf. Cover with a lid and simmer gently for about 25 minutes.

Remove the bay leaf and transfer the kidneys turbigo to a serving dish. Garnish with croûtons and chopped parsley.

CALF'S LIVER WITH ORANGE SAUCE

Liver and kidneys are very popular in France – I love them too! Liver is usually cooked very quickly, so that it is browned on the outside and pink in the middle. Cook it a little more if you like, but do not overcook and toughen it.

Serves 6

INGREDIENTS

90g/3oz butter

1 large piece of calf's liver about 680-900g/1½-2lbs, cut into slices

4 oranges (2 squeezed for their juice, and the remaining 2 peeled of skin and pith and cut into thin slices)

280ml/½ pint veal or chicken stock

Salt and freshly ground black pepper

1 tbsp freshly chopped chives

Heat most of the butter in a large frying pan and cook the liver briskly until browned on both sides. Remove the liver and keep it warm on a plate over a saucepan of boiling water. Wipe the pan out to remove any excess fat, add the juice of 2 of the oranges and cook rapidly, scraping the bottom of the pan with a wooden spoon to mix any remaining liver sediment into the juice. Add the veal stock and salt and pepper, bring to the boil and add the orange slices. Allow the orange to colour slightly, then remove the slices with a fork and place them on the liver.

Remove the pan from the heat and stir in the remaining butter. Season to taste. Serve the sauce poured over the liver and sliced oranges, and garnish with the chopped chives.

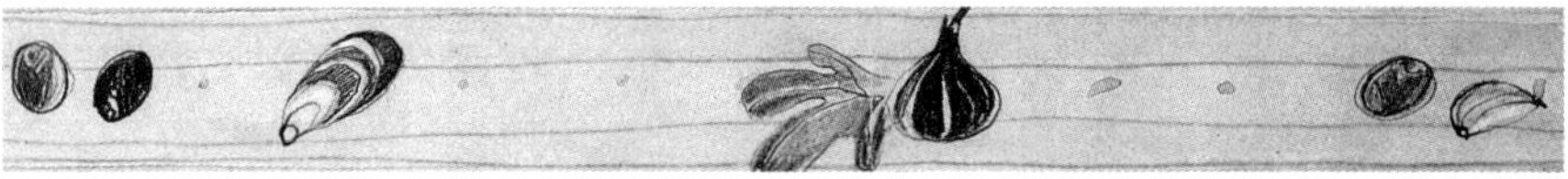

STEAMED CALF'S LIVER

Another simple but rich recipe for liver. Steam the liver quite briskly – or you could slice the liver and pan-fry or grill it if preferred. I think the liver is more attractive with a browned exterior!

Serves 4

INGREDIENTS
1 sprig fresh tarragon
90ml/3fl oz wine vinegar
2 shallots, chopped
1 tsp peppercorns, lightly crushed
280ml/½ pint whipping cream, whipped
90ml/3fl oz milk
1kg/2¼lbs whole calf's liver, trimmed and skin removed
Salt and freshly ground black pepper
60g/2oz butter

Chop half the tarragon finely and put it in a saucepan with the vinegar, shallots and peppercorns. Heat, and allow to boil until the vinegar has almost completely evaporated, then whisk in the cream and the milk. Allow to reduce slightly and then strain the sauce through a fine sieve. Remove from the heat, and keep warm.

Steam the whole liver on a bed of the remaining tarragon until still just pink in the centre: this will take 10-15 minutes. Season with salt and pepper. Slice the liver thinly and place on a heated serving plate. Put the sauce back onto a gentle heat and whisk in the butter. Season and serve immediately.

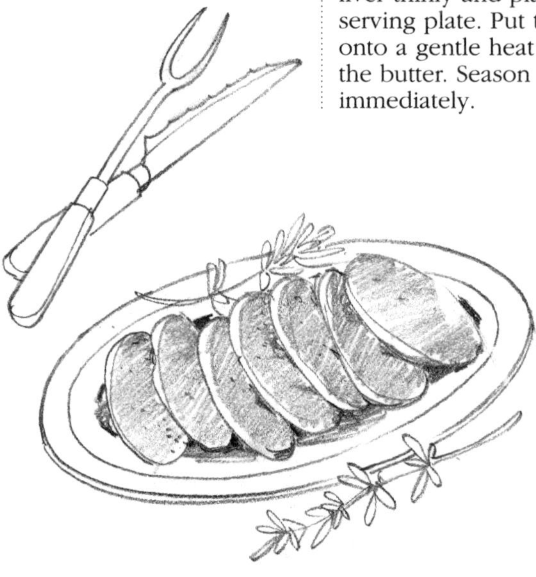

KIDNEY FRICASSÉE

Sautéed calves' kidney in a sweet, creamy sauce. Lambs' kidneys may be easier to obtain than calves kidneys and they work just as well in this recipe. If any blood runs from the kidneys, drain it away and do not add it to the sauce. Serve with rice.

Serves 6

INGREDIENTS

900g/2lbs calves' or lambs' kidneys
1 tbsp olive oil
250g/9oz mushrooms, sliced
Salt and white pepper
2 tbsps Madeira
200ml/7fl oz veal stock
90ml/3fl oz double cream

Prepare the kidney by cutting into small cubes, removing the core. Heat the oil in a frying pan and sauté the kidney and the mushrooms until cooked to your liking. Season with salt and pepper. Remove the kidney and keep warm. Deglaze the frying pan with the Madeira allowing it to almost evaporate, then stir in the stock and reduce by half. Add the cream and salt and pepper to taste. Put the kidney back into the sauce and heat through. Serve hot.

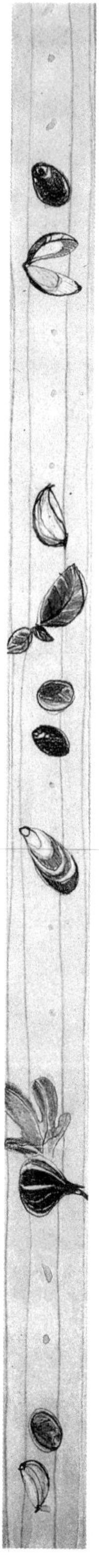

VEGETABLES

In common with most cooks I just love being in France and shopping in the French markets. The range of fruits and vegetables is absolutely astounding, all displayed in top condition. It is impossible for me to spend even a few hours on French soil without shopping for at least 1 kilo of chicory and half a dozen Breton artichokes!

Vegetables and salads are seldom eaten with the main course in France but are enjoyed separately, between the main course and the dessert. This allows the vegetables to be savoured in their own right, rather than merely as an accompaniment to fill up the plate!

Seasonal Variety

Modern supermarkets have certainly helped in the shrinking of our ever diminishing world, but they have also offered us the benefit of a huge array of produce from many lands, available throughout the year. What makes the French style of vegetable cookery so different is that most people prefer to shop in markets, where they are offered and buy the best of what is in season. How often do you actually notice the basket of fresh walnuts in your supermarket in October? In a French market you cannot but be aware of the huge displays of nuts and so you know that, at that moment, there is something special about walnuts. Oh, for such reliability here in England! I find that my local market will sell almost the same range of produce as the supermarket in an attempt to compete, rather than concentrating on what is fresh and best.

Garlic – A Taste of France

There are several vegetables without which it is impossible to even contemplate the preparation of a French meal! The first of these must surely be garlic. The most important thing to remember is that the fresher the garlic, the milder its flavour. The huge bulbs of very juicy garlic available in late summer and early autumn have a flavour which is less likely to remain with you through to the following day than the smaller, drier cloves one might buy and use in the spring! Also remember that the redder the skin of the garlic the stronger the flavour – it is almost like a social acceptability warning system! Cooked garlic is less pungent than raw (it's the practice of using garlic in butter and salad dressings that will make you unpopular with non-garlic eaters!) and dried, granules or garlic salt bear no relation to the real thing!

Artichokes – My Favourite Vegetable

Globe artichokes, as I have already mentioned, are one of the vegetables that I always seek out when I am in France. I am certain that many people are deterred from eating some of the slightly more exotic vegetables, such as artichokes, simply because they are not certain how to prepare them. I think that artichokes are one of the most romantic of foods – one will generally serve two people, so there is an intimacy in the eating, and they take some time to consume, allowing you to relax and enjoy a glass of wine. I generally serve an artichoke as a starter. Trim the stalk close to the globe and snip off the tops of the leaves, especially if they are spiky and non-finger friendly! Boil the artichoke for about 40 minutes, according to size, until dark green in colour. The outer leaves will pull off easily once the artichoke is ready.

A Licence to Flirt!

Serve the artichoke with vinaigrette, garlic mayonnaise or melted butter. Take off the leaves and dip the bases, drawing them through your teeth to remove the fleshy part. It will take you some time to work your way through to the centre, the hairy choke. Remove this with a teaspoon and divide the remaining fleshy heart, the fond, between the diners. This is the *pièce de la rèsistance* of the artichoke and should be liberally coated in the remaining butter or dressing before eating! Delicious! Of course, the French for 'flirt' is *fond d'artichoke!* As a respectable married woman I must point out that that is not why I am so addicted to the vegetable . . .

The other vegetable that I have really appreciated since first travelling to France is endive, more commonly known as chicory. Even now I am not keen on raw chicory, which is often served in salads with orange, as it has a very bitter taste. Roasted in a hot oven with a little finely chopped onion, salt, pepper and olive oil it is quite different and utterly delicious!

FENNEL RAMEKINS

These light fennel moulds are easy to prepare and cook and, with their aniseed flavour, make an original dish. Be certain that the fennel is well cooked and that you have exactly 570ml/1 pint of the purée.

Serves 6

INGREDIENTS

900g/2lbs fennel bulbs, cut into quarters
1.14 litres/2 pints milk
4 eggs, beaten
1 tbsp Pernod, or other aniseed alcohol
200ml/7fl oz double cream
Salt and freshly ground black pepper
A little butter for greasing

Preheat the oven to 160°C/325°F/Gas Mark 3. Cut away any hard patches from the fennel and discard them. Poach the fennel in the milk for about 30 minutes, then leave to drain well. Once the fennel is well drained, place the quarters in a liquidiser or food processor and blend until smooth – this should give about 570ml/1 pint of pulp. If necessary, make up to the required amount by adding some of the cooking milk. Whisk in the eggs, Pernod, cream, salt and pepper.

Butter 6 ramekin dishes and fill them three quarters full with the fennel mixture. Place the ramekins in a high-sided dish, add water to come halfway up the sides of the ramekins, and cook in the preheated oven for 30-40 minutes. To serve, turn the baked fennel out of the ramekins on to heated serving plates.

STUFFED ARTICHOKE HEARTS

When artichokes are at the height of their season and relatively cheap, they make a most exotic vegetable to stuff. Cut away most of the leaves and boil the artichokes for 20–30 minutes. Canned artichokes are convenient, but a poor substitute for fresh.

Serves 6

INGREDIENTS
6 large fresh or canned globe artichoke hearts
Juice of 1 lemon
225g/8oz mushrooms, finely chopped
Knob of butter
120g/4oz ham finely chopped
120g/4oz Jambon de Bayonne, or similar smoked ham, chopped
Salt and freshly ground black pepper
120g/4oz cheese, grated

Sauce
30g/1oz butter
30g/1oz flour
280ml/½ pint milk
Pinch of nutmeg
Salt and freshly ground black pepper
3 tbsps single cream

Preheat the oven to 200°C/400°F/Gas Mark 6. Cook the fresh artichoke hearts in boiling water with the juice of half the lemon until tender. Drain well and remove the hairy 'choke'. Coat the hearts with the remaining lemon juice and set aside. Cook the mushrooms with the knob of butter over a high heat for a few minutes, until their juices run. Remove from the heat and discard the juices. Stir the chopped hams and salt and pepper into the mushrooms and heat through completely.

To make the sauce, melt the butter in a saucepan, beat in the flour, and cook for 1 minute. Gradually add the milk and beat continuously until the mixture boils and thickens. Reduce the heat and cook for a further 2 minutes. Remove from the heat and stir in the nutmeg, salt and pepper and cream.

Stir most of the cheese into the ham and mushroom mixture. Pile this mixture on to the artichoke hearts. Grease an ovenproof dish, place the prepared artichokes in it, spoon the sauce over each artichoke and scatter with the remaining grated cheese. Cook in the hot oven for 10-15 minutes, until well browned on the top.

ARTICHAUTS AÏOLI ARTICHOKES WITH GARLIC MAYONNAISE

This is one of my favourite ways of serving artichokes – so simple and so delicious! Garlic butter is a good alternative, but this rich garlic mayonnaise is best!

Serves 4

INGREDIENTS
4 medium-sized globe artichokes
1 slice lemon
1 bay leaf
Pinch of salt

Sauce Aïoli
2 egg yolks
2 cloves garlic, crushed
Salt, freshly ground black pepper and lemon juice to taste
280ml/½ pint olive oil
Chervil leaves to garnish

To prepare the artichokes, break off the stems and twist to remove any tough fibres. Trim the base so that the artichokes will stand upright. Trim the points from all the leaves and wash the artichokes well. Bring a large saucepan or stock pot full of water to the boil with the slice of lemon and bay leaf. Add a pinch of salt and, when the water is boiling, add the artichokes. Allow to cook for 25 minutes over a moderate heat. While the artichokes are cooking, prepare the sauce.

Whisk the egg yolks and garlic with a pinch of salt and pepper in a deep bowl or in a liquidiser or food processor. Add the olive oil a few drops at a time while whisking by hand, or in a thin, steady stream with the machine running. If preparing the sauce by hand, once half the oil is added, the remainder may be added in a thin steady stream. Add a little lemon juice once the sauce becomes very thick. When all the oil has been added, adjust the seasoning and add more lemon juice to taste.

When the artichokes are cooked, the bottom leaves will pull away easily. Remove them from the water with a draining spoon and drain upside–down on absorbent kitchen paper or in a colander. Allow to cool slightly and serve with the sauce aïoli. Garnish with chervil.

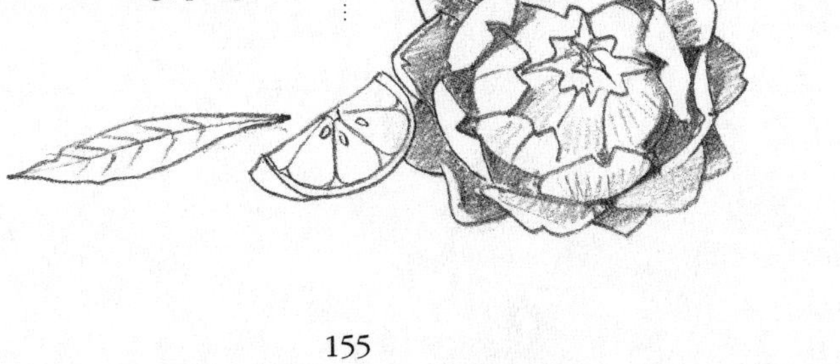

POMMES DE TERRE BOULANGÈRE
BAKERY STYLE POTATOES

These potatoes are well-known as Pommes de Terre Boulangère – baked by the baker! They go well with any meat dish and are almost good enough to eat by themselves!

Serves 4-6

INGREDIENTS
900g/2lbs potatoes, thinly sliced
1 large onion, finely chopped
Salt and freshly ground black pepper
430ml/¾ pint hot stock
60g/2oz butter

Preheat the oven to 180°C/350°F/Gas Mark 4. Generously butter a wide, shallow baking dish. Arrange a layer of potatoes in the base of the dish, then a little onion and salt and pepper. Continue until you have used all the ingredients, finishing with a layer of potatoes and seasoning.

Pour in the stock and dot the surface with knobs of butter. Place the dish on the highest shelf of the oven and cook for 45 minutes. The potatoes should be soft when pierced with a sharp knife or skewer and the top should be golden-brown. They can be finished off under a hot grill, if necessary, for extra browning.

COURGETTES 'AU GRATIN'

'Au gratin' simply means in a cheese sauce. It is a very popular way of cooking vegetables and fish – use a roux thickened cheese sauce, or a cream and cheese mixture as in this recipe.

Serves 4

INGREDIENTS
460g/1lb courgettes
½ tsp salt
150ml/¼ pint water
1 egg, lightly beaten
150ml/¼ pint double cream
2 tbsps Gruyère cheese, grated (Cheddar is a good alternative)
Freshly ground black pepper
15g/½oz butter

Preheat the oven to 200°C/400°F/Gas Mark 6. Wipe the courgettes, trim the ends and cut them into 1.25cm/½ inch slices. Place them in a saucepan with the salt and water. Cook over a moderate heat until almost all the water has evaporated.

Mix together the egg, cream and 1 tablespoon of the cheese in a small bowl. Season with black pepper.

Carefully place the courgettes in a gratin dish or shallow ovenproof dish. Pour the cream mixture over and top with the rest of the cheese. Dot with butter and bake in the oven for about 10 minutes, or until just set and golden brown.

SAUERKRAUT SALAD

This recipe clearly shows the German influence on the cooking of Alsace, the region from which the salad comes. Fresh sauerkraut has more texture than canned, so I prefer to use it when possible.

Serves 6

INGREDIENTS

5 tbsps olive oil
2 tbsps wine vinegar
1 tsp sugar
Freshly ground black pepper
1 tsp cinnamon
½ tsp salt
680g/1½lbs cooked, fresh sauerkraut, soaked for 2 hours
Juice of 1 lemon
1 red apple, diced
2 small onions, chopped
2 carrots, grated

Mix the oil, vinegar, sugar, pepper, cinnamon and salt together in a large salad bowl, until all the sugar and salt has dissolved. Wash the sauerkraut in cold water and drain well. Remove any excess moisture with a dry tea-towel. Cut the dry sauerkraut into even lengths. Pour the lemon juice over the apple, onions and carrot. Mix all the ingredients together in the salad bowl, tossing them in the dressing.

BUTTERED CABBAGE

I am always grateful for new ideas for cooking cabbage! The addition of bacon and onion makes a very special dish from a rather humble ingredient.

Serves 8

INGREDIENTS

1.4kg/3lbs cabbage, shredded
120g/4oz goose or other poultry dripping or lard
225g/8oz smoked bacon, chopped
1 medium onion, chopped
120g/4oz butter
Salt and freshly ground black pepper

Blanch the cabbage in boiling salted water for 4-5 minutes. Drain well. Melt the dripping or lard in a large frying pan. Add the bacon, onion and cabbage, and stir well. Cover and cook over a very gentle heat for 20 minutes, then stir in the butter and cook for a further 20 minutes, covered. Season to taste and serve in a heated serving dish.

CARROTS WITH ONIONS & BACON

This is a rich and colourful dish of carrots. New season's carrots have a sweet flavour and are the best for this dish. On the other hand, it is an excellent way of making dull old carrots a little more exciting.

Serves 6

INGREDIENTS

3 tbsps goose or poultry dripping
1.4kg/3lbs carrots, finely sliced into rounds
460g/1lb onions, finely sliced
1 bouquet garni
340g/¾lb smoked bacon, diced
1 tsp sugar
½ tsp cinnamon
Salt and freshly ground black pepper

Gently melt the goose or poultry dripping in a large, heavy-based frying pan, then increase the heat and sauté the carrots, onions and bouquet garni. Shake the pan from time to time to prevent the vegetables from sticking. Once the vegetables begin to colour, reduce the heat, cover and cook for 25-30 minutes.

Blanch the bacon in boiling water for 3 minutes, drain well and add to the carrot mixture. Sprinkle with the sugar and cinnamon, cover and continue to cook until very tender. Season with salt and pepper before serving.

POMMES DARPHIN AUX OIGNONS
POTATO PATTIES WITH ONIONS

These little potato patties could be baked in bun tins or ramekins. Oil the tins well so that the patties will release easily for a good presentation.

Serves 4

INGREDIENTS
4 large potatoes
1 onion, finely chopped
1 tbsp freshly chopped herbs
Salt and freshly ground black pepper

Preheat the oven to 200°C/400°F/Gas Mark 6. Cut the potatoes into small matchsticks, either by hand or in a machine. Stir the onion and herbs into the potato.

Oil 4 small moulds and divide the mixture even between them. Season each patty with salt and pepper. Cook in the preheated oven for 15 minutes. Turn the patties out on to a baking sheet and brown the tops under a hot grill if necessary.

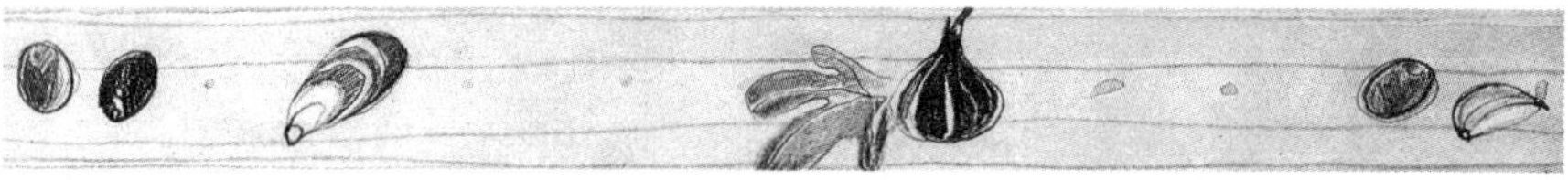

BAKED AUBERGINES

Aubergines cooked in olive oil always remind me of summer holidays and sunshine. Be certain to wash the aubergines thoroughly to remove all the salt, or the dish will be spoiled.

Serves 6

INGREDIENTS

4 medium-sized aubergines, sliced
Salt and freshly ground black pepper
90ml/3fl oz olive oil
2 cloves garlic
1kg/2¼lbs tomatoes, seeded and sliced
1 bay leaf
Pinch of thyme
1 tbsp freshly chopped parsley
120g/4oz cheese, grated

Spread the aubergine slices out on a plate and sprinkle liberally with salt, or layer them with salt in a colander. Allow to stand for about 30 minutes then rinse thoroughly and dry on absorbent kitchen paper.

Preheat the oven to 200°C/400°F/Gas Mark 6. Fry the aubergines in 4 tbsps of the olive oil over a high heat, but take care not to let them burn. Remove the slices from the frying pan and drain on absorbent kitchen paper. Retain any oil left in the pan and add the remaining olive oil and cook the garlic cloves. Cook gently so that they flavour the oil. Remove the garlic and discard it. Add the tomatoes, bay leaf and thyme and cook for 20 minutes. Remove the bay leaf.

Pour half the tomato mixture into the base of an ovenproof dish, sprinkle over the parsley and add a little salt and pepper. Lay the slices of aubergine over the tomatoes, followed by half of the cheese, then the rest of the tomato mixture and lastly the remaining cheese. Cook in a hot oven for 15-20 minutes, until well browned.

BROCCOLI 'AU GRATIN'

This broccoli 'au gratin' uses a cheese sauce based on a roux. For cooking "au gratin" using a cream sauce see the recipe for Courgettes au Gratin.

Serves 6

INGREDIENTS
3 large heads broccoli, trimmed
30g/1oz butter
30g/1oz flour
280ml/½ pint milk
4 tbsps double cream
Pinch of nutmeg
Salt and freshly ground black pepper
60g/2oz cheese, grated

Preheat the oven to 200°C/400°F/Gas Mark 6. Cook the broccoli in boiling salted water until almost cooked but slightly crisp. Plunge them immediately into cold water to stop them from cooking any further, then drain well.

Make a white sauce in a saucepan by melting the butter and stirring in the flour, cook for 1 minute and then gradually add the milk. Stir until boiling and thickened. Remove the sauce from the heat, and stir in the cream, nutmeg, salt, pepper and half the cheese.

Chop the broccoli roughly with a sharp knife, mix it with the sauce and pour into an ovenproof dish. Sprinkle with the remaining cheese and cook in the hot oven until the top is crisp and brown – about 15 minutes.

POTATOES DAUPHINOIS

This is a luxurious way of cooking potatoes. Bake them slowly to start with, so that they soften and absorb the cream, and then crisp them in the oven at its highest setting.

Serves 4–6

INGREDIENTS
30g/1oz butter
2kg/4½lbs potatoes, sliced
570ml/1 pint single cream
1 clove garlic, crushed
Salt and freshly ground black pepper
Pinch of nutmeg
120g/4oz cheese, grated

Preheat the oven to 160°C/325°F/Gas Mark 3. Grease an ovenproof dish with the butter and fill with the sliced potatoes. Mix the cream with the garlic, salt and pepper and nutmeg, then pour the cream over the potato. Cook gently in a warm oven for 1½ hours, adding a little milk if the cream does not cover the potatoes.

Remove the potatoes from the oven. Set the oven to its highest temperature, and sprinkle the grated cheese over the potatoes. Cook in the hot oven until crisp and golden brown, about 15 minutes.

TURNIPS IN CREAM

Turnips are often undervalued, but I think they are delicious. I often serve them in a parsley sauce – this recipe produces a much more luxurious dish.

Serves 8

Ingredients

1kg/2¼lbs turnips
225g/8oz smoked bacon, diced
280ml/½ pint single cream
Salt and freshly ground black pepper
Pinch of nutmeg

Cut the turnips into small cubes and blanch them for 2 minutes in lightly salted boiling water. Remove and drain well. Place the turnip, bacon, cream, salt, pepper and a pinch of nutmeg in a large saucepan and cook over a gentle heat until the turnip has absorbed quite a lot of the cream. Serve piping hot on small individual plates.

SPRING SALAD

This is a striking and spicy salad, an unusual flavour being added by the horseradish. Remember that preparing horseradish might make you cry!

Serves 6

INGREDIENTS
1 lettuce, washed and shredded
1 cucumber, sliced
1 horseradish root, washed and evenly sliced
3 tomatoes, seeded and sliced
340g/12oz can tuna fish, drained
12 black olives, pitted
6 spring onions
A few sprigs of fresh mint
200ml/7fl oz olive oil
3 drops Tabasco
90ml/3fl oz wine vinegar
Salt and freshly ground black pepper

Prepare all the vegetables, taking special care with the cucumber and horseradish as these will be the centrepiece of your finished salad. On a large, round serving plate, arrange the tuna fish in a round and then form a rose shape on top of the fish by interlacing cucumber and horseradish slices. In a liquidiser or food processor, purée the olives, spring onions, mint leaves, olive oil, Tabasco, vinegar and salt and pepper until smooth. Place the shredded lettuce around the rose, followed by the tomatoes, and then pour the olive and mint mixture over the salad.

SURPRISE POTATOES

Choose large new potatoes for this dish and take care not to break the skins when scooping out the centres.

Serves 8

INGREDIENTS

1 red pepper, seeded and cut into thin strips
1 tbsp olive oil
1.8kg/4lbs new potatoes, steamed (but not peeled)
120g/4oz butter
200ml/7fl oz double cream
Salt and freshly ground black pepper

Preheat the oven to 200°C/400°F/Gas Mark 6. Cook the pepper strips in the olive oil over a high heat for a few minutes. Remove from the heat and set aside. Cut the potatoes in half and remove the centres with a teaspoon. Leave enough potato with the skins for them to hold their shape. Work the butter, cream, salt and pepper into the potato that you have scooped out, then stir in the pepper strips. Spoon the mixture back into the skins and warm through in the hot oven for 5-8 minutes. Serve piping hot.

SALADE PAYSANNE

This salad can be made from any selection of vegetables – your favourites or those in season. Cut some of the vegetables diagonally to make the salad as attractive as possible.

Serves 6

INGREDIENTS
4 spring onions
½ cucumber
3 carrots
6 large tomatoes
10 button mushrooms
3 stalks celery
1 green pepper, seeded and chopped
15–20 tiny cauliflower florets
15–20 radishes
1 tbsp chopped watercress, or mustard and cress
2 sprigs coriander leaf, or parsley
½ tsp salt
½ tsp freshly ground black pepper
2 tbsps cider vinegar
1 tbsp lemon juice
4 tbsps olive or vegetable oil
Pinch of mustard powder
Sugar to taste
8 lettuce leaves for garnish

Trim the spring onions and cut them diagonally into thin slices. Peel the cucumber and quarter it lengthways. Use a sharp knife to remove the soft, seedy centre, discard this, and dice the remaining flesh. Peel the carrots and slice them thinly, cutting them diagonally with a sharp knife.

Cut a small cross into the skin of each tomato, and plunge into boiling water for 30 seconds. Remove the tomatoes and carefully peel away the blanched skin from the fruit. Quarter the skinned tomatoes and cut away the tough green stalk. Thinly slice the mushrooms and celery. Cut the pepper in half lengthways and remove all the seeds and the white pith. Discard this, and chop the flesh. Break the cauliflower florets into small pieces, quarter the radishes, and roughly chop the watercress, or mustard and cress, along with the coriander leaves or parsley.

Mix together all the remaining ingredients, except the lettuce leaves. Whisk thoroughly using a fork, or balloon whisk, until the mixture becomes a thick, cloudy dressing.

Arrange the lettuce leaves on a serving dish, and pile the prepared vegetables on top. Spoon a little of the dressing over the salad just before serving and hand the remainder separately in a small jug.

GLAZED VEGETABLES

This method of preparing vegetables is especially suited to root vegetables such as carrots, turnips, swedes and parsnips. However, the addition of cucumber makes a most refreshing contrast.

Serves 6

INGREDIENTS
460g/1lb carrots
1 large cucumber
460g/1lb turnips
60g/2oz butter
9 sugar cubes
Salt and freshly ground black pepper

Wash and peel the vegetables as necessary. Cut them into long oval shapes with a sharp knife. Melt the butter in a large frying pan and add the vegetables, sugar and salt and pepper. Stir, adding just enough water to cover the vegetables. Cook over a high heat, allowing the water to evaporate. Leave the vegetables to caramelise a little and then serve. Care should be taken as some vegetables cook more quickly than others. If time permits, cook the vegetables separately.

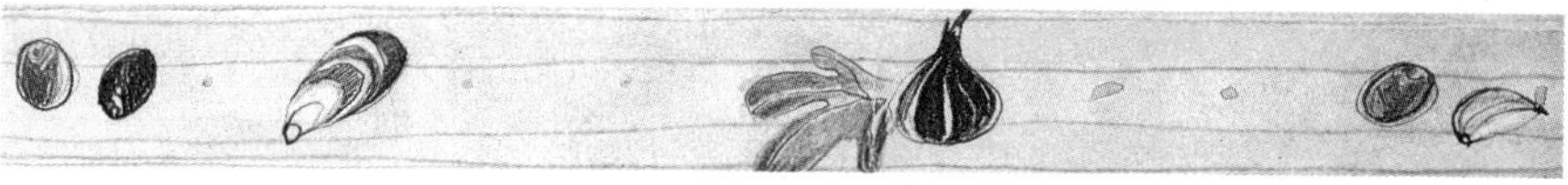

HARICOTS VERTS À LA PROVENÇALE
FRENCH BEANS PROVENÇALE

This dish is traditionally made with haricots verts – French beans. It is, however, a wonderful way of cooking runner beans towards the end of their season.

Serves 7

Ingredients
60g/2oz butter
3 tbsps olive oil
1 bouquet garni
1 clove garlic, chopped
6 large tomatoes, seeded and chopped
2 onions, chopped
1.4kg/3lbs French beans, topped and tailed
Salt and freshly ground black pepper

Garnish
½ clove garlic, finely chopped
1 tbsp freshly chopped parsley

Heat the butter and oil together in a large frying pan. Add the bouquet garni, garlic, tomatoes and onions and cook for 20-30 minutes or until very soft.

Cook the beans in boiling salted water until just cooked but still crisp. Run them immediately under cold water to stop further cooking. Drain well and add salt and pepper. Remove the bouquet garni from the tomatoes. Serve the beans on a bed of the tomato purée and garnish with the chopped garlic and parsley.

CARROT PURÉE

Vegetable purées come and go in food fashions around the world but they have always been popular in France. I sometimes add a little grated cheese to the purée.

Serves 6

INGREDIENTS
1.4kg/3lbs carrots, sliced
1 tbsp ground cinnamon
120g/4oz butter
150ml/¼ pint double cream
Salt and freshly ground black pepper
Juice of half a lemon

Cook the carrots in boiling salted water until soft. Drain well then push the carrots through a fine sieve or blend to a smooth purée in a liquidiser or food processor. Return the purée to the heat in a clean saucepan, and stir in the cinnamon, butter, cream and salt and pepper. Beat well with a wooden spoon and heat through. Serve in a preheated dish with the lemon juice squeezed over.

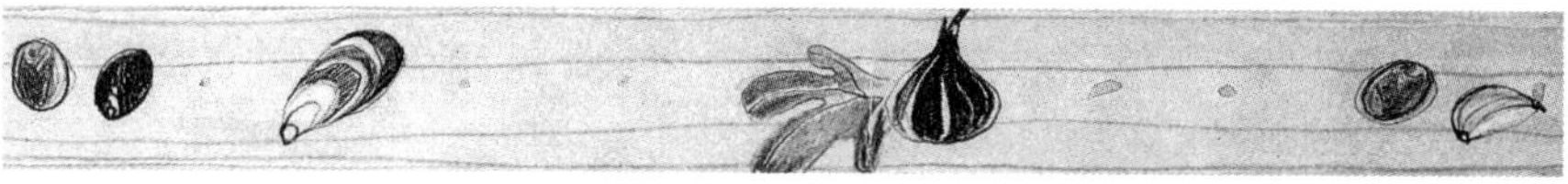

RATATOUILLE

Ratatouille is one of the most famous French vegetable dishes, a stew of Mediterranean vegetables. There are many different recipes – in this one the vegetables are fried, which helps them to retain their individual flavours.

Serves 6

Ingredients
3 aubergines, diced
4 courgettes, diced
1 red pepper, seeded and diced
1 green pepper, seeded and diced
12 baby onions
4 large tomatoes, seeded and diced
3 cloves garlic, chopped
1.14 litres/2 pints olive oil
Sprig thyme
1 bay leaf
Salt and freshly ground black pepper

Prepare all the vegetables, taking care to retain all the juice from the tomatoes when removing the seeds. Set the oil to heat in a large frying pan. Fry the aubergines in the oil until just brown. Remove and drain well. Leave on absorbent kitchen paper. Fry the courgettes and drain well, then fry the red and green peppers and drain well. Finally, fry the baby onions and drain well.

Place all the cooked vegetables in a heavy-based saucepan with the garlic, tomatoes, any tomato juice recovered during seeding, the sprig of thyme, bay leaf, salt and pepper, 2 tbsps water and 2 tbsps of the frying oil. Cover and cook for 45 minutes-1 hour over a very low heat. Stir from time to time to prevent sticking. Remove the thyme and bay leaf before serving and add salt and pepper to taste.

TOMATES À LA LANGUEDOCIENNE
TOMATOES FROM LANGUEDOC

This dish is a celebration of ripe tomatoes and fresh juicy garlic. I could easily eat this on toast for lunch!

Serves 4

Ingredients
4 large ripe tomatoes
Salt and freshly ground black pepper
2 tbsps olive oil
1 clove garlic, crushed
2 slices white bread, crusts removed
1 tbsp freshly chopped parsley
2 tsps freshly chopped thyme or marjoram

Cut the tomatoes in half and score the cut surface. Sprinkle with salt and leave upside-down in a colander to drain. Allow the tomatoes to drain for 1-2 hours. Rinse the tomatoes and scoop out most of the juice and pulp. Mix the olive oil and garlic together and brush both sides of the bread with the mixture, leaving it to soften. Chop the herbs and bread together until well mixed.

Press the filling into the tomatoes and sprinkle with the remaining garlic and olive oil mixture. Cook the tomatoes in an ovenproof dish under a preheated grill at low heat for 5 minutes, then raise the dish or the heat to brown the tomatoes on top. Serve immediately.

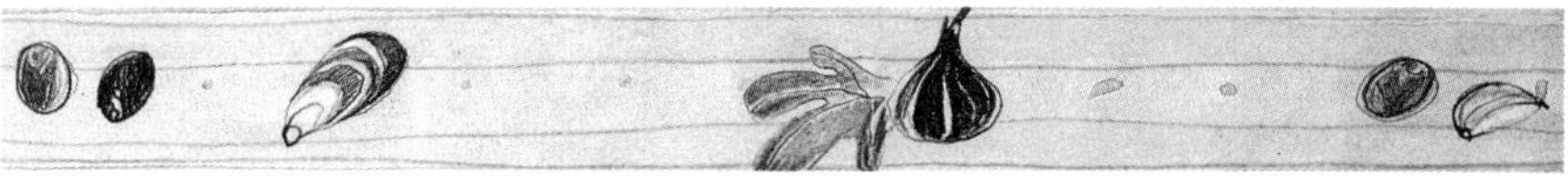

BROAD BEANS WITH HAM

I am often surprised by how few French people know of broad beans – one of my favourite vegetables. Yet they grow happily and plentifully in France, as this recipe from Touraine, the fertile lands south of the Loire, shows.

Serves 6

INGREDIENTS

900g/2lbs shelled broad beans
150ml/¼ pint double cream
60g/2oz ham, cut into strips
Salt and freshly ground black pepper
1 tbsp freshly chopped parsley or chervil

If using fresh beans, remove them from their pods. Cook the beans in boiling salted water until tender, drain and keep them warm. Combine the cream and ham in a small saucepan. Add a pinch of salt and pepper and bring to the boil. Boil rapidly for 5 minutes to thicken the cream. If wished, peel the outer skins from the beans before tossing them with the cream and ham. Add parsley or chervil, adjust the seasoning and reheat if necessary. Serve immediately.

PETITS POIS BONNE FEMME

This recipe title quite literally means 'housewive's peas'. Oh! that all housewives were so inventive!! Baby onions and crispy bacon provide contrasts in both flavour and texture.

Serves 6

INGREDIENTS
400g/14oz smoked bacon, chopped
60g/2oz butter
1kg/2¼lbs fresh peas (about 3kg/7lbs in the pod)
12 baby onions
2 tsps sugar
Salt and freshly ground black pepper

Cook the chopped bacon in half the butter, then add the peas and just enough water to cover. Heat until just cooked, then drain well. Glaze the baby onions. To do this, cover them with water in a clean saucepan, add the sugar and the remaining butter, and season with salt and pepper. Cook over a moderate heat until the juice has reduced and is lightly coating the onions (like a syrup). Add the baby onions to the peas just before serving.

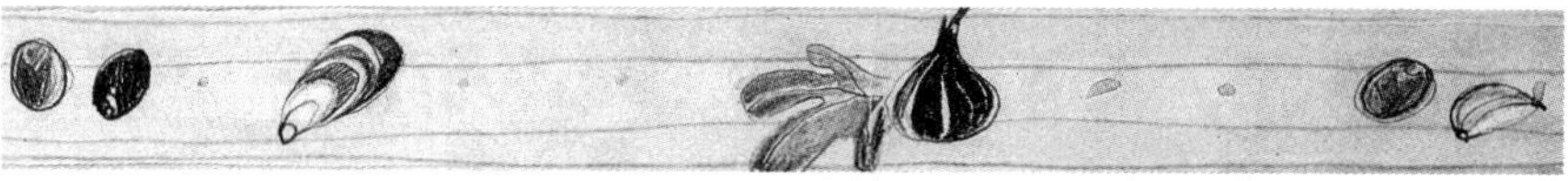

SALADE NIÇOISE

As with so many of the classic dishes of the world, the definitive recipe for Salade Niçoise is muddled with the many popular variations on a theme. I sometimes use green beans and cold potatoes in place of the cucumber and artichokes, but it is delicious any way!

Serves 4–6

INGREDIENTS
1 Cos lettuce
2 hard-boiled eggs, quartered
2 large tomatoes, quartered
6 anchovy fillets
10 black olives, pitted
1 tbsp capers
¼ cucumber, diced but not peeled
200g/7oz can tuna fish, drained
4 large artichoke hearts, quartered

Dressing
90ml/3fl oz olive oil
2 tbsps white or red wine vinegar
½ clove garlic, crushed
1 tsp mustard
Salt, freshly ground black pepper and lemon juice

Wash the lettuce well, pat dry and break into bite-sized pieces. Prepare the remaining salad ingredients and toss with the lettuce in a large bowl, taking care not to break up the eggs. Mix the dressing ingredients together and whisk until well emulsified. Pour the dressing over the salad just before serving.

FRENCH BEANS WITH ONION

Such a simple recipe and such a delicious result! This method could be used for cooking any type of green bean; runner, broad, green or French.

Serves 4-6

INGREDIENTS
460g/1lb French beans
1 medium onion
30g/1oz butter
Salt and freshly ground black pepper

Top and tail the beans, then cook them whole in boiling salted water for about 8–10 minutes. Meanwhile, finely chop the onion. Melt the butter and fry the onion until lightly brown. Drain the beans and toss them over the heat to dry. Pour the butter and onions over the beans and season with salt and pepper. Serve immediately.

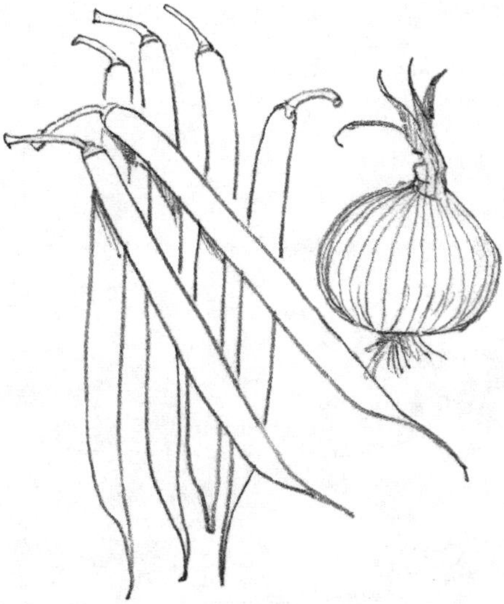

SALADE BRESSE

The rich blue cheese dressing makes this a sophisticated salad. It is at its best in the autumn, when the new crop of walnuts reaches the market stalls.

Serves 4-6

INGREDIENTS

1 head radicchio leaves, separated and washed
1 Cos lettuce, washed
1 bunch of lamb's lettuce or watercress, washed
120g/4oz cherry tomatoes, halved and cored
4 chicken breasts, cooked, skinned and thinly sliced
120g/4oz Bresse Bleu, or other blue cheese, cut into small pieces
16 small pickled gherkins, thinly sliced
60g/2oz walnut halves
2 tbsps vegetable oil
2 tbsps walnut oil
2 tsps white wine vinegar
175ml/6fl oz fromage frais
2 tsps freshly chopped tarragon
Salt and freshly ground black pepper

Tear the radicchio and Cos lettuce into bite–sized pieces. Pull apart the lamb's lettuce, but leave the leaves whole. If using watercress, remove any thick stems and yellow leaves. Toss the lettuces together in a large salad bowl. Arrange the tomatoes, chicken, cheese, gherkins and walnuts on top of the lettuce and mix gently.

Place the oils and vinegar together in a small bowl and whisk well, until they are thick. Fold in the fromage frais and the tarragon. Whisk well, then season to taste. Drizzle some of the dressing over the salad before serving. Place the remaining dressing in a small jug and hand it round separately.

PETITS POIS À LA FRANÇAISE

It is most unusual to cook lettuce, but this is a classic way of cooking peas. The shredded lettuce really does add to the dish and make it special.

Serves 6

INGREDIENTS
1kg/2¼lbs fresh peas (about 3kg/7lbs in the pod)
60g/2oz butter
1 lettuce, finely shredded
6 onions, finely chopped
2 tsps sugar
1 bouquet garni
Salt and freshly ground black pepper
2 carrots, finely diced

Rinse the peas under cold running water and leave them to drain. Melt the butter in a heavy-based saucepan and gently cook the peas, lettuce, onions, sugar, bouquet garni and salt and pepper for 5 minutes. Increase the heat, add 2.5cm/1 inch of water, bring to the boil and add the carrots. Cover the saucepan, reduce the heat to very low and cook for 15-20 minutes, or until the peas are cooked through. Remove the bouquet garni and serve.

DESSERTS

Desserts are an excuse. An excuse for what? Well, that's up to you, but for most of us desserts are an excuse for self indulgence, for wallowing in gorgeous confections that might well be bad for us but really finish a meal perfectly, leaving us comforted and replete!

For simplicity, choose ripe fresh fruit in a state of utter perfection and serve it, when appropriate, in a bowl of iced water. If you like to fiddle, spending time in the kitchen on intricate decorations, then some desserts will suit your inclinations. There will also be an ideal dessert for you to make if you prefer something simple and fruity that can be prepared in advance, such as an ice cream, a sorbet or a cold soufflé. And, if you are a chocoholic, what better excuse could there be for spending a little time in the kitchen than producing the most heavenly, wicked chocolate tart?

Simple Desserts in Heavenly Combinations

The ingredients for desserts are seldom complicated in themselves. There are a few standard compilations which are used extensively, especially in classic French desserts, which are simple to make but add amazing depths. *Crème pâtisserie* or pastry cream, caramel and praline are almost basic ingredients in so many recipes but might appear off-putting if you are not already an experienced cook. Do not allow these things to daunt you – they are all easy to prepare and will open the door to many of the great desserts of France if you can master them. Recipes for all of these can be found in the chapter on Basic Recipes at the back of this book.

Three Basic Skills

Crème pâtisserie is a rich, set egg custard and may be used in place of cream to fill pastry tarts before covering them with fresh fruits in season. It may be flavoured with a little liqueur and may also be lightened by the addition of just a little whipped cream. I love using this pastry cream and find it much less rich than desserts which are stuffed full of dairy cream.

Caramel is used in so many ways – burnt over custards, pulled into strands over choux buns, set and crushed in ice creams and for dipping ripe fruits for petits fours. It is so versatile. Praline is one stage on from caramel and includes nuts. It is crushed or ground before being added to creamy fillings or being used for decoration.

Sugar, the Basic Ingredient of Desserts

Desserts didn't really become popular until the late fifteenth and sixteenth centuries. Until that time honey was the main sweetener in use throughout Europe but sugar had, in fact, been in common use in India since the fifth century B.C. When first introduced to Europe, sugar was very expensive and the inclusion of any sweet dishes at banquets and parties was more to show the extent of the host's wealth than anything else.

France, with it's great tradition of experimentation in gastronomy, was able to lead in the development of many of the classic desserts now common throughout the world.

Some of My Favourite Puds!

Yes, a lot of them are French and most of them are included in this chapter! crême brulée, a rich custard with a burnt sugar topping, chocolate roulade, strawberry tarts, profiteroles, Normandy apple tarts and tarte au citron – I love them all! Sheer and utter self-indulgence maybe, but each and every one of them provides the perfect ending to a meal. Of course, which meal may hold the key to the ultimate success of the pudding – don't choose something heavy and rich to serve after a rich main course. Selecting a dessert is just as important as planning the other courses of your meal.

A Secret Society?

Two sisters by the name of Tatin ran the Hôtel Terminus in Lamotte-Beuvron, in the Loire. They often produced an apple tart and one day, by mistake, one of the sisters placed the apples which she had caramelised with butter and sugar into a pie tin which she had omitted to line with pastry. Rather than scoop it all out, she simply covered the apples with the pastry and inverted the tart onto a serving plate when cooked. Like so many great discoveries Tarte Tatin was a mistake! It is now, however, one of the most popular and fashionable desserts in France – there is even a Tarte Tatin Society in the sisters' home town with an avidly enthusiastic membership.

GRAPEFRUIT AND WILD STRAWBERRY DUO

Lightly poached fresh grapefruit with a fresh wild strawberry sauce make a simple yet stylish dessert.

Serves 6

INGREDIENTS

5 grapefruit
280ml/½ pint Muscat wine
60g/2oz sugar
400g/14oz wild strawberries, washed and hulled

Peel four of the grapefruits, removing all the white pith and cut into quarters. Squeeze the remaining grapefruit for its juice.

Place the Muscat wine and half the sugar in a saucepan and allow to reduce by half. Add the grapefruit quarters and poach for 1 minute, then remove them using a slotted spoon. Stir in the juice of the fifth grapefruit. Crush the wild strawberries with the remaining sugar, spread this paste over a serving plate, lay the poached grapefruit quarters over the paste and serve the sauce separately in a small serving jug.

BANANAS IN ORANGE SAUCE

The delicious caramel orange sauce makes this a perfect dish hot or cold. To obtain a really authentic flavour, use French Rivesaltes in place of the sherry.

Serves 6

INGREDIENTS
30g/1oz butter
3 tbsps sugar
1 tbsp cream sherry
2 tbsps orange liqueur
Juice of 2 oranges
6 large bananas, peeled

In a heavy-based saucepan, melt the butter and sugar together over a gentle heat. When dissolved, increase the heat and boil the mixture until a white caramel forms. Carefully stir in the sherry, liqueur and orange juice, and allow the mixture to reduce a little. Cut the bananas into even slices and add them to the sauce.

With a tablespoon, remove the sauce-coated bananas and arrange them on individual plates. Make rose shapes by interlacing the bananas, then pour over the remaining sauce.

GATEAUX GIENNOIS

A nutty-flavoured, fluffy-topped tart, with a surprise raspberry centre.

Serves 4

INGREDIENTS
225g/8oz sweet pastry (see recipe)
3 egg yolks
120g/4oz sugar
75g/2½oz shelled walnuts, ground
2 egg whites, stiffly beaten
4 tbsps raspberry jam

Preheat the oven to 180°C/350°F/Gas Mark 4. Roll out the pastry on a lightly floured surface and use it to line 4 individual pie tins, pricking the bases and sides with a fork. Beat together the egg yolks and the sugar until pale, then stir in the ground walnuts. Gently incorporate the beaten egg whites using a metal spoon. Place 1 tbsp of jam in the base of each tart and spoon over the mixture dividing it evenly between the 4 tarts. Cook in the preheated oven until the pastry is cooked and the filling lightly puffed, about 20 minutes. Serve as soon as possible.

CRÈME BRÛLÉE

I always tease a friend of mine who invariably serves crème brûlée whenever we eat with her – but we don't really mind because it is delicious! Fresh fruit may be hidden under the custard.

Serves 6-8

Ingredients
4 egg yolks
1 tsp cornflour
60g/2oz caster sugar
Vanilla essence
280ml/½ pint double cream
280ml/½ pint single cream

Caramel
90g/3oz granulated sugar
3 tbsps water

Blend the egg yolks, cornflour, caster sugar and a little vanilla essence together in a bowl. Heat the creams until they reach boiling point, then pour on to the egg yolks, stirring all the time with a wooden spoon. Mix well and return the mixture to the saucepan over a gentle heat. Stir continually until the cream has thickened. This will take a few minutes. If the cream overheats, remove the pan from the heat and beat until it becomes smooth. Divide the mixture between six ramekins or pour it into a soufflé dish. Leave to cool, then cover with plastic wrap and refrigerate overnight.

Place the sugar and water in a pan over a low heat until the sugar dissolves. Boil until golden brown in colour. Pour the caramel carefully over the creams and chill until required.

Alternatively, sprinkle the top of the chilled cream with granulated sugar, covering the surface completely with the sugar. Place under a very hot grill until the sugar melts and turns golden, but do not allow it to burn. Return the crème brûlée to the refrigerator until needed.

CŒUR À LA CRÈME

These creamy desserts are traditionally made in heart–shaped moulds, making a very romantic pud! However, individual ramekins work just as well.

Serves 6

INGREDIENTS
460g/1lb curd cheese
120g/4oz caster sugar
Grated rind of 1 lemon
3 large ripe peaches
Juice of ½ lemon
2 tbsps orange liqueur
4 tbsps dry white wine
6 ripe strawberries for decoration

Combine the curd cheese, sugar and lemon rind together in a bowl (this can also be done in a food processor). Press the mixture into six moulds, and chill for 4-6 hours.

Meanwhile, skin, halve and stone the peaches. Liquidise the flesh and mix in the lemon juice, orange liqueur and dry white wine.

When you are ready to serve, turn the moulds out onto flat plates and spoon a little peach purée around each one. Partly slice each strawberry and fan them out to decorate each plate.

Many different fruits could be used with the cœur à la crème – plums and raspberries both work well and blueberries, although not so traditional, make a dramatic contrast in colour.

CHOCOLATE ROULADE

A roulade is merely a culinary term for a roll with a filling. Roulades may be sweet or savoury, but chocolate is my favourite!

Serves 8–10

Ingredients
5 eggs, separated
225g/8oz caster sugar
175g/6oz plain chocolate
2 tbsps water
Icing sugar

Filling
280ml/½ pint double cream flavoured with a liqueur or vanilla essence, lightly whipped

Preheat the oven to 180°C/350°F/Gas Mark 4. Line a shallow Swiss roll tin with greased greaseproof or silicone paper.

Separate the eggs and beat the yolks into the sugar until the mixture is pale yellow. Melt the chocolate with the water in a bowl over a pan of water over gentle heat, or melt in a microwave on defrost for 6 minutes. Beat the melted chocolate into the egg yolk and sugar mixture. Whip the egg whites until very firm and fold them into the chocolate mixture. Pour the mixture into the prepared tin and gently level the surface. Bake the roulade for 20 minutes.

Remove the roulade from the oven and cool slightly. Cover with a clean tea-towel wrung out in cold water; this is to prevent a hard crust from forming. Place the roulade in the refrigerator and leave for 12-24 hours.

Lay a piece of greaseproof paper on a flat surface and dust with icing sugar. Tip out the roulade upside down on to the prepared paper and remove the oiled greaseproof paper. Cover the roulade with the whipped cream and roll it up like a Swiss roll. Dust with a little extra icing sugar. Keep in the refrigerator until ready to serve.

This roulade freezes very well and thaws in just a few hours.

FRESH FRUIT CREAM

This is an unusual but simple dessert, memorable yet quick to prepare. The creamy custard topping is browned quickly under a hot grill – a variation on crème brûlée.

Serves 6

INGREDIENTS

280ml/½ pint crème pâtissière (see recipe)
2 tbsps Kirsch
225ml/8fl oz whipping cream, whipped with 30g/1oz sugar
Seasonal fresh fruit, peeled, pitted, sliced or cubed (enough for 6 servings)

Preheat the oven to 190°C/375°F/Gas Mark 5. Gently mix together the crème pâtissière, Kirsch and 2 tbsps of the whipped cream then, using a metal spoon, gently fold in the remaining cream.

Arrange the fruit in an ovenproof dish, spoon over the topping and cook for 10 minutes in the preheated oven. Transfer to a hot grill, and allow the top to crisp until brown. Serve immediately.

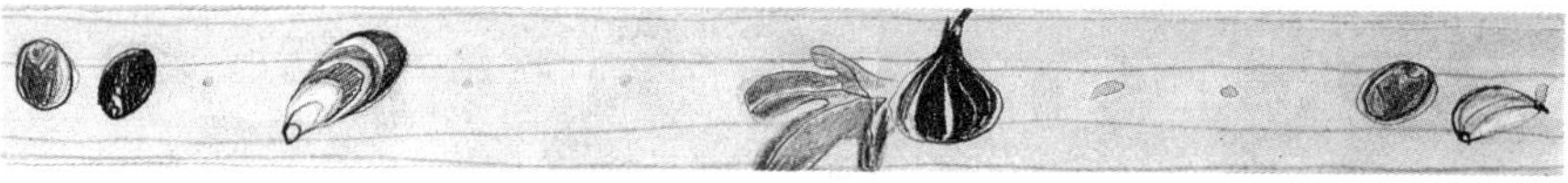

JALOUSIE DES FRUITES
OPEN FRUIT TART

This was one of the first classic French desserts that I was taught at cookery college to practise using puff or flaky pastry. It is simple, spectacular and delicious.

Serves 4-6

Ingredients

400g/14oz puff pastry

Egg for glazing

Assorted fruit e.g. 3-4 peaches, 120g/4oz cherries, small punnet strawberries, 120g/4oz grapes

3 tbsps jam (apricot is good as it does not mask the colour of the fruits, but if all red fruits are used, use raspberry jam)

1 tbsp lemon juice

Preheat the oven to 220°C/425°F/Gas Mark 7. Roll out the pastry into a large rectangle approximately 6mm/¼ inch thick. Using a sharp knife, cut strips of pastry 2.5cm/1 inch wide from all sides of the rectangle. Transfer the rectangle to a dampened baking sheet and, with cold water, moisten the edges. Lay the strips along the edges (make sure they are evenly trimmed) and press down lightly to seal the surfaces. Prick the base with a fork, leaving the edging strips plain. Flute or crimp the edges with a knife or finger and thumb, and glaze with a little beaten egg. Place the pastry in the preheated oven for 15-20 minutes, until risen and golden. Remove from the oven and cool on a wire rack.

To fill: Slice the peaches. Pit the cherries, seed the grapes and leave the strawberries whole. Place the fruit carefully in rows according to size or colour. Meanwhile, place the jam in a small saucepan together with the lemon juice and bring to the boil, stirring continually. Allow to cool but not to reset. (If it is too thick, add a little boiling water.) Using a pastry brush, liberally coat the fruit with the jam glaze.

Do not assemble this dessert too far in advance – leave it as late as possible, not more than 1-2 hours before serving.

As an alternative, fill the base with 280ml/½ pint of crème pâtissière (see recipe) or whipped double cream and top with the fruits.

CRÊPES SUZETTE

This is the classic dish of paper-thin pancakes flamed and flavoured with orange liqueur. With a well used and trusted frying pan this is a very easy and impressive recipe to prepare.

Serves 4 (Allow about 3 crêpes per person)

INGREDIENTS

Crêpe Batter

430ml/¾ pint milk and water mixed
4 eggs
Pinch of salt
225g/8oz plain flour, sifted
1 tbsp sugar
4 tbsps melted butter or oil

Orange Butter

60g/2oz butter
60g/2oz sugar
Grated rind of 1 orange
1-2 tbsps Grand Marnier or Curaçao

To Flame

2 tbsps brandy
2 tbsps Grand Marnier or Curaçao
30-45g/1-1½oz butter

Place all the ingredients for the crêpes in a liquidiser or food processor and blend for about 1 minute, pushing down the ingredients from the sides occasionally. Process a few seconds more to blend thoroughly. Leave, covered, in a cool place for 30 minutes-1 hour. The consistency of the batter should be that of thin cream. Add more milk if necessary. Brush a crêpe pan or small frying pan lightly with oil and place over a high heat. When a slight haze forms, pour a large spoonful of the batter into the pan and swirl the pan to cover the base. Pour out any excess into a separate bowl. Cook on one side until just beginning to brown around the edges. Turn over and cook on the other side until lightly speckled with brown. Slide each crêpe on to a plate and repeat using the remaining batter. Reheat the pan occasionally in between cooking the crêpes. The amount of batter should make 12 crêpes.

For the orange butter, cream together the butter, sugar and grated orange rind until light and fluffy. Add the orange liqueur and spread a little of this orange butter on one side of each crêpe.

To flame the crêpes, place the brandy and orange liqueur in a small saucepan ready to flame them at the last moment.

Melt the butter in a large frying pan, add a crêpe, orange butter side down, and cook very quickly for half a minute. Fold in half and half again into the traditional triangular shape and put to one side of the pan. Repeat until all the crêpes are cooked.

Heat the liqueur in the small saucepan, set alight and pour over the crêpes. Serve at once.

PEACH MELBA

One of the classic deserts, created by Escoffier in 1893 to celebrate the soprano Dame Nellie Melba. Served with a raspberry coulis this dessert is one of summer's pleasures.

Serves 6

INGREDIENTS
175g/6oz sugar
Juice of half a lemon
1 tbsp Kirsch
460g/1lb fresh raspberries
6 fresh, ripe peaches, skinned, or whole canned peaches in syrup
570ml/1 pint vanilla ice cream

Place 280ml/½ pint of water in a saucepan with the sugar, lemon juice, Kirsch and the raspberries. Boil briskly for 5 minutes, then set aside to cool. Once cool, blend in a liquidiser or food processor until smooth then pass the purée through a fine sieve. Chill in the refrigerator.

Place each peach in a small bowl, add a scoop of ice cream and spoon over a little of the raspberry sauce.

APPLES WITH MUSCAT DE BEAUMES DE VENISE

Muscat de Beaumes de Venise is one of the best known of all dessert wines. It is the most marvellous ingredient to cook with for special occasions.

Serves 4

INGREDIENTS
60g/2oz butter
4 Golden Delicious apples, peeled and quartered
60g/2oz sugar
3 tbsps currants
120ml/4fl oz Muscat de Beaumes de Venise
1 tsp cinnamon

Melt the butter in a large frying pan and cook the apples until lightly browned, then add the sugar and allow to caramelise slightly. Sprinkle with the currants and cook for a few seconds more. Add the wine and boil until slightly reduced, then sprinkle with the cinnamon and serve immediately.

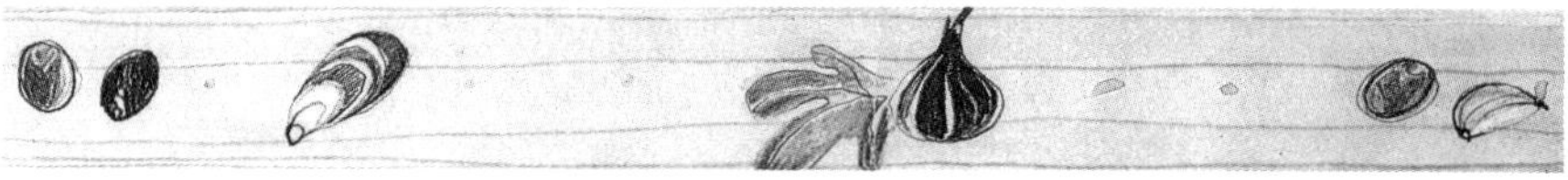

FRESH FRUIT IN RED WINE SYRUP

Pears are traditionally prepared by poaching in red wine. This method creates a contemporary variation of the classic recipe and uses fruits that do not require poaching or cooking.

Serves 8

INGREDIENTS

1 litre/1¾ pints light red wine (Beaujolais or similar)
200ml/7fl oz water
460g/1lb sugar
1 clove
Zest of 1 orange
1 stick cinnamon
A selection of fresh fruit, peeled, pitted, sliced or halved as necessary

Make a syrup by boiling together the wine, water, sugar, clove, orange zest and cinnamon for at least 30 minutes. Remove from the heat and set aside to cool. Chill in the refrigerator.

Prepare the fruit and arrange it on a serving dish or in a bowl. Remove the cinnamon and clove from the syrup and pour the chilled liquid over the fruit. Serve.

SOUFFLÉ AU CITRON FROID

This is one of my favourite desserts – it is very easy to make (although it requires several bowls) and has a refreshing tang. Use double or whipping cream – I find the latter gives a lighter result. You should be able to write a four-lettered word across the egg yolk mixture when it is sufficiently well beaten and thickened.

Serves 6

INGREDIENTS

3 eggs, separated
175g/6oz sugar
Grated rind and juice of 2 small lemons
1 tbsp gelatine soaked in 3-4 tbsps hot water
175ml/6fl oz cream, lightly whipped

Decoration

150ml/¼ pint cream, whipped
Finely chopped almonds or pistachios
Thin strips lemon rind or lemon twists

Tie a double thickness of greaseproof paper around a soufflé dish to stand about 7.5cm/3 inches above the rim of the dish, and set to one side.

Beat the egg yolks in a large bowl. Add the sugar gradually and the lemon rind and juice. Set the bowl over a pan of hot water and whisk until the mixture is thick and leaves a ribbon trail. Remove the bowl from the heat and whisk for a few minutes longer. Dissolve the gelatine in the water until clear, pour it into the lemon mixture and stir thoroughly. Set the bowl over ice and stir until beginning to thicken.

Whip the egg whites until stiff but not dry and fold into the lemon mixture along with the lightly whipped cream. Pour into the prepared soufflé dish and chill in the refrigerator until the soufflé is set. To decorate, peel off the paper carefully and thinly spread some of the cream on the sides of the soufflé. Press finely chopped nuts into the cream. Pipe the remaining cream into rosettes on top of the soufflé and decorate with strips of rind or lemon twists.

MOUSSE AU CHOCOLAT BASQUE
BASQUE CHOCOLATE MOUSSE

A rich, thick chocolate mousse – very simple to make and an all-time favourite dessert with everyone. Use a good quality chocolate with at least 50 per cent cocoa solids.

Serves 7

INGREDIENTS
175g/6oz plain chocolate
75ml/2½fl oz water
1 tbsp butter
2 tbsps rum
3 eggs, separated
Whipped cream and chocolate curls to decorate, optional

Chop or break the chocolate into small pieces and combine with the water in a bowl over a heavy-based saucepan of water. Cook over a very gentle heat so that the chocolate and water form a thick cream. Remove the bowl from the heat, allow to cool slightly and then beat in the butter. Add the rum and beat in the egg yolks one at a time.

Whisk the egg whites until stiff but not dry and fold them gently into the chocolate mixture. Pour into small pots or ramekins and chill for at least 2–3 hours. Finish with whipped cream and chocolate curls, if wished.

CRÊPES AU CHOCOLATE FRAMBOISES

PANCAKES WITH CHOCOLATE RASPBERRIES

The French do not only use crêpes to make Crêpes Suzettes!! These rich, thin pancakes may be filled with almost any fruit and sauce of your choice – I like to use fresh raspberries in season, in place of the jam.

Serves 6

INGREDIENTS

Crêpe Batter

430ml/¾ pint milk and water mixed
4 eggs
Pinch of salt
225g/8oz plain flour, sifted
1 tbsp sugar
4 tbsps melted butter or oil

Filling

225g/8oz plain dessert chocolate, grated
120g/4oz seedless raspberry jam

Decoration

Whipped cream and chopped, toasted hazelnuts

Preheat the oven to 180°C/350°F/Gas Mark 4. Place all the ingredients for the crêpes in a liquidiser or food processor and blend for about 1 minute, pushing down the ingredients from the sides occasionally. Process for a few seconds more to blend thoroughly. Leave, . covered, in a cool place for 30 minutes - 1 hour. The consistency of the batter should be that of thin cream. Add more milk if necessary. Brush a crêpe pan or small frying pan lightly with oil and place over a high heat. When a slight haze forms, pour a large spoonful of the batter into the pan and swirl the pan to cover the base. Pour out any excess into a separate bowl. Cook on one side until just beginning to brown around the edges. Turn over and cook on the other side until lightly speckled with brown. Slide each crêpe onto a plate and repeat using the remaining batter. Reheat the pan occasionally in between cooking the crêpes. The amount of batter should make 12 crêpes.

As the crêpes are cooked, sprinkle them evenly with grated chocolate and divide the raspberry jam amongst them. Roll them up so that the jam shows at the ends, or fold into triangles. Reheat in the preheated oven for about 10 minutes before serving. Top with whipped cream and a sprinkling of toasted nuts.

FRENCH APPLE FLAN

The most striking thing about French Apple Flans is the attractive arrangement of the sliced apple, and the fact that dessert apples are most commonly used, not cooking apples. I leave the skin on the apples if it is red.

Serves 6

INGREDIENTS
90g/3oz plain flour
90g/3oz self-raising flour
60g/2oz butter
60g/2oz margarine
30g/1oz sifted icing sugar
Cold water (about 2-3 tbsps)

Filling
4 tbsps apricot jam
2 tbsps water
Juice of 1 small lemon
570g/1¼lbs dessert apples
1 tbsp caster sugar

Preheat the oven to 200°C/400°F/Gas Mark 6. Place the flours in a bowl then rub in the fats until the mixture resembles fine breadcrumbs. Stir in the icing sugar. Mix to form a firm but pliable dough with cold water. Knead the dough lightly on a floured surface until smooth. Roll out the pastry and use it to line a 23-24cm/9-9½ inch loose-bottomed French fluted flan tin.

To prepare the filling, boil together the jam and water for 2-3 minutes, stirring constantly. Sieve the glaze into a cup to cool. Squeeze the lemon juice into a bowl. Peel, core and thinly slice the apples straight into the lemon juice. Arrange the apple slices neatly in the pastry case, overlapping them in circles, and sprinkle with the sugar. Place the flan on a baking sheet and cook in the preheated oven for about 35 minutes. Whilst still hot, brush the flan with the apricot glaze. Serve warm with thick cream.

FLOATING ISLANDS

This might sound a bit daunting, but the poaching of meringue islands is very straightforward. Just take care not to over-cook them, as they will dissolve away to nothing!

Serves 4

INGREDIENTS
6 egg whites
Pinch of salt
120g/4oz caster sugar
430ml/¾ pint milk
430ml/¾ pint water
430ml/¾ pint Egg Custard Sauce (see recipe)
2 tbsps crushed Praline (see recipe)

Whisk the egg whites with a pinch of salt until light and foamy. Add half the sugar and whisk until almost stiff. Add the remaining sugar and continue whisking until stiff peaks form. Heat the milk and water together over a moderate heat. Place the meringue mixture in a forcing bag without a nozzle and squeeze large 'islands' of meringue out on to a spatula. If you do not have a bag, simply use a tablespoon to scoop out the islands and drop them directly into the hot milk and water. Lower each meringue island onto the hot milk and water on the spatula and poach gently for about 2 minutes, turning once – the cooking time will depend on the size of the islands. Do not poach for too long or they will dissolve.

Remove the islands from the milk and water using a slotted spoon and leave them to drain and cool on a wire rack. To serve, divide the custard sauce between four serving plates, place the meringue islands on top, and sprinkle with the crushed praline before serving.

BRIOCHE FRENCH TOASTS

This not a true classic dish, but I am certain that you will recognise the method! This makes a quick and economical family dessert.

Serves 4

INGREDIENTS
4 small brioches
4 tbsps double cream
3 eggs
1 tbsp sugar
1 tsp orange flower water
2 tbsps melted butter
Icing sugar
Egg Custard Sauce (see recipe)

Cut each small brioche into three slices. Beat together the cream, eggs, sugar and orange flower water. Dip each brioche slice quickly into the cream and egg mixture, making sure both sides are coated.

Heat a little of the butter at a time and sauté the dipped slices in batches, cooking the toasts for about 2 minutes on each side, until golden brown. Serve each batch immediately, sprinkled with a little sifted icing sugar and surrounded by egg custard sauce.

FRAISES ESCOFFIER
STRAWBERRIES ESCOFFIER

The combination of strawberries and sweet oranges is delicious and well worthy of the great chef Escoffier.

Serves 4

INGREDIENTS
900g/2lbs strawberries
2 oranges
60g/2oz sugar cubes
75ml/2½fl oz Grand Marnier

Hull and slice the strawberries, and peel, removing all the white pith, and slice the oranges. Mash half the strawberries with the sugar and Grand Marnier, then stir in the remaining strawberries and the oranges. Chill the fruit mixture for 1 hour, then serve in individual glasses.

CHOCOLATE SOUFFLÉ

Hot soufflés create a big impression on friends and family, and are actually very easy to prepare. Chocolate soufflé is lighter than chocolate mousse. Both are definitely classic French desserts.

Serves 4

INGREDIENTS
Melted butter
Sugar
2 eggs, one separated
120g/4oz caster sugar
2 tbsps flour
1 heaped tbsp cocoa powder
225ml/8fl oz milk
4 egg whites
Pinch of salt
Icing sugar

Preheat the oven to 200°C/400°F/Gas Mark 6. Grease four ramekins with the melted butter, and sprinkle with sugar, shaking out any excess.

Beat one whole egg plus one egg white with the sugar and then beat in the flour and the cocoa powder. Bring the milk to the boil in a small saucepan then pour it over the egg mixture, stirring continuously. Return the mixture to the saucepan and stir it continuously over a low heat until it has thickened and is just coming to the boil. Remove from the heat and allow to cool. When cool, add the remaining egg yolk and mix well.

Beat the egg whites with a pinch of salt until stiff. Mix a little of the egg white into the soufflé mixture to lighten it and then fold in the remaining egg whites gently but thoroughly. Fill the ramekins with the soufflé mixture and bake in the preheated hot oven for about 20 minutes, until well risen and firm. Remove from the oven, sprinkle quickly with icing sugar and serve immediately, before the soufflés fall.

BLACKCURRANT SORBET

Sorbets and water ices are popular everywhere. This sorbet makes a light dessert but sorbets are more commonly used in France to clear the palette between savoury courses.

Serves 4-6

INGREDIENTS
900g/2lbs fresh or thawed frozen blackcurrants
225g/8oz sugar
280ml/½ pint water
2 egg whites

Place all the ingredients, except the egg whites, in a saucepan, and cook slowly over a low heat for 15 minutes. Press the fruit mixture through a sieve, then pour into a freezer-proof container with a lid. Freeze until mushy. Whisk the egg whites until firm and fold into the partly frozen blackcurrant mixture. Return to the freezer until almost frozen. If the sorbet becomes completely frozen and hard, leave it in the refrigerator for 15 minutes to soften before serving.

PEAR CHARLOTTE

I always like to use fresh fruit in season (pears and peaches both work well in this dessert) but canned fruit may also be used. This is another of the classic desserts that looks daunting but is really simple to make.

Serves 6

INGREIDNTS

4 large ripe pears, peeled and cored
2 tbsps sugar
150ml/¼ pint apple juice
150ml/¼ pint fromage frais
2 tbsps gelatine
4 tbsps pear liqueur
4 tbsps water
225ml/8fl oz double cream
14 boudoir biscuits
Melted chocolate, to decorate

Cut one pear into dice and set aside. In a liquidiser or food processor, blend the remaining pears with the sugar and apple juice. Add the fromage frais, and mix well.

Soften the gelatine in a little cold water then place in a saucepan with 2 tbsps of the pear liqueur and 2 tbsps of the water. Stir over a gentle heat to dissolve. Do not allow the gelatine mixture to boil. Mix the dissolved gelatine into the fromage frais and pear purée. Whisk the cream until thick, then fold into the pear mixture. Carefully fold in the reserved diced pear.

Mix together the remaining 2 tbsps pear liqueur and 2 tbsps water, and brush over the boudoir biscuits, then use them to line the bottom and sides of a charlotte mould or straight-sided cake tin. Turn the pear mousse into the lined mould. Leave to set in the refrigerator for at least 3 hours. Turn out and serve chilled, decorated with a little melted chocolate.

STRAWBERRY MOUSSE

Light and refreshing, this is a classic dessert that enjoys enduring popularity.

Serves 4

Ingredients
225ml/8fl oz water
175g/6oz caster sugar
900g/2lbs fresh or frozen strawberries
2 tbsps gelatine
150ml/¼ pint double cream
Mint leaves, to decorate

Boil the water and sugar together for about 7 minutes to make a light syrup. Add 570g/1lb of strawberries and set aside for about 15 minutes. Purée the mixture in a liquidiser or food processor, then pass the purée through a sieve to remove the seeds.

Dice six of the remaining strawberries. Soften the gelatine in a little cold water. Measure out 150ml/¼ pint of the purée, reheat if not hot, then add the gelatine and stir until it has completely dissolved. Add the diced strawberry then set aside until the mixture is cool but not set. Whisk the cream until thick. Fold it gently but thoroughly into the cooled strawberry mixture. Pour the mousse into four individual moulds or one large mould and leave to set in the refrigerator for at least 2 hours.

Prepare a purée from the remaining strawberries. Place them in a saucepan with 150ml/¼ pint of water and cook until soft. Press the pulp through a sieve and sweeten to taste with sugar if necessary. Cool and chill. To serve, unmould the mousses onto individual serving plates and surround with the strawberry purée. Decorate the mousses with small mint leaves.

PRUNE & ARMAGNAC MOUSSE

Prunes and Armagnac are both traditional foods in south west France. The main prune area is around Agen, where the best prunes in the world are produced – well, that's my opinion! Delicious!

Serves 4

INGREDIENTS

225g/8oz fromage frais
280ml/½ pint Egg Custard Sauce (see recipe)
120g/4oz pitted prunes
1 tbsp gelatine
2 tbsps Armagnac, or to taste
150ml/¼ pint double cream

Place the fromage frais and the custard sauce in a liquidiser or food processor. Add the prunes and process quickly. Turn the mixture out into a bowl. Soften the gelatine in a little cold water then place in a small saucepan with a further 2 tbsps water and the Armagnac. Heat gently and stir until the gelatine dissolves. Pour the gelatine into the fromage frais mixture and beat together well. Whisk the cream until light and fluffy, then fold it gently into the prune custard.

Divide the mousse between four individual moulds or ramekins and leave to set in the refrigerator for at least 2 hours. Unmould and serve chilled.

PEAR OMELETTE

Sweet omelettes are quite delicious. They are a classic French dessert and deserve to be more popular outside France. Make certain that you use unsalted butter for cooking the omelette!

Serves 4

INGREDIENTS
4-5 ripe pears
12 eggs
2 tbsps double cream
2 tbsps caster sugar
Pinch of ground cloves
Oil or unsalted butter

Peel, core and dice the pears. Beat the eggs with the cream and sugar. Add a pinch of ground cloves and stir in the pears.

Heat about 2 tbsps of oil or butter in a large omelette pan. When hot, pour in the egg mixture. Stir the mixture a little in the pan, then cook for a few minutes until set. Shake the omelette loose and flip it over, as for a pancake, and cook on the other side. Serve warm, cut into quarters.

CHILLED SOUFFLÉS GRAND MARNIER

Grand Marnier is one of the best known of French liqueurs. It has an orange flavour and is excellent for cooking – as well as for drinking!

Serves 4

INGREDIENTS
6 egg yolks
120g/4oz caster sugar
3 tbsps Grand Marnier
6 egg whites
150ml/¼ pint whipping cream

Prepare four ramekins: fix a 'collar' of waxed paper around each one, securing the paper with tape or string. Place the egg yolks, sugar, Grand Marnier and 1 tbsp of water in a bowl set over a saucepan of simmering water and beat until the mixture forms a ribbon, a thick thread, if dropped from a spoon. Remove from the heat and continue to beat until the mixture has cooled. Whisk the egg whites until stiff peaks form, whisk the cream until light and fluffy.

Fold the egg whites gently into the egg mixture, so as not to lose any of the volume, and then fold in the whipped cream. Divide the mixture between the prepared ramekins. Leave to chill in the refrigerator for at least 3 hours, or until set. Remove the paper collars from the ramekins just before serving.

FROZEN NOUGAT

Nougat is very typically French, either as a dessert or as a sweet confectionary. It is very sweet, so only serve small portions.

Serves 6

INGREDIENTS
90g/3oz raisins
90g/3oz candied fruit
2 tbsps coconut liqueur
120g/4oz honey
4 tsps caster sugar
2 tbsps water
4 egg whites
150ml/¼ pint double cream
2 tbsps crushed Praline

Soak the raisins and the candied fruit in the coconut liqueur for at least 30 minutes. Boil the honey, sugar and water in a small saucepan for 3-4 minutes to obtain a thick syrup. Whisk the egg whites until very stiff. Gradually add the hot syrup to the egg whites, beating continuously until a thick, smooth meringue is obtained. Whisk the cream and fold it gently into the meringue mixture, then add the crushed praline, the raisins and the candied fruit together with their marinade; stir gently.

Line a loaf tin with waxed paper, pour in the nougat mixture and place in the freezer for 24 hours. To serve, turn the frozen nougat out of the loaf tin, remove the waxed paper and cut the nougat into wedges or slices. Serve immediately.

CHOUX PUFFS WITH CARAMEL ICE CREAM

I don't know why no-one makes a commercial caramel ice cream – it is so delicious! This is a modern variation of an old classic – a new way of serving profiteroles.

Serves 4

INGREDIENTS

Ice cream

120g/4oz sugar
2 tbsps water
120ml/4fl oz water
225ml/8fl oz Egg Custard Sauce (see recipe)

Choux Pastry

2 tbsps melted butter
120ml/4fl oz water
1 tsp sugar
Pinch of salt
75g/2½oz plain flour
2 eggs, beaten

Make a caramel using the 120g/4oz sugar and the 2 tbsps water (for method see recipe in Basic Recipes). When the sugar has caramelised, add the extra water, return to the heat for 1 minute and stir to mix, then set aside to cool. Combine the cooled caramel with the custard sauce, stirring together thoroughly, then pour into an ice cream maker and process until the ice cream sets. Alternatively, pour the mixture into a freezing tray and freeze for 2 hours. Remove from the freezer, thoroughly beat the part-frozen mixture and then replace in the freezer until set.

Preheat the oven to 200°C/400°F/Gas Mark 6. Lightly grease a baking sheet. To make the choux pastry, bring the butter, the remaining water and sugar and salt to the boil in a medium-sized saucepan. When the mixture is boiling, tip in all the flour at once, beat thoroughly and cook the paste, stirring continuously, for another 2 minutes. Remove the paste from the heat, add the first egg and beat until well mixed. Add the second egg, beating well to obtain a smooth, elastic dough – do not add all the egg if it is not required. Place the pastry in a forcing bag with a plain metal nozzle. Pipe balls of choux pastry on to a greased baking sheet. Dip a fork in beaten egg and slightly flatten each of the balls. Bake in the preheated oven for about 20 minutes, or until lightly browned and well puffed. Remove from the oven and set aside to cool.

Cut open the base of each choux puff and spoon or pipe in a little of the caramel ice cream. Chill the filled puffs for 30 minutes in the freezer before serving.

PEARS 'BELLE HÉLÈNE'

This is probably the best-known of all the classic French desserts featuring pears – it is utterly delicious, a perfect combination of ingredients. The first recipe for Pears 'Belle Hélène' may not have included ice cream – but I like it!

Serves 4

INGREDIENTS
4 large ripe pears
120g/4oz good plain chocolate
120ml/4fl oz milk
2 tsps sugar
4 scoops vanilla ice cream
1 tbsp toasted, slivered almonds

Cut the pears in half lengthways and remove all the seeds from the centre with a melon baller or teaspoon. Cut each half pear into even slices lengthways.

Melt the chocolate with the milk and sugar in a bowl set over a saucepan of hot water. Mix together well. Fan out each pear on a serving plate. Pour the chocolate sauce around the edges, top with a scoop of ice cream and sprinkle with the almonds. Serve immediately.

STRAWBERRY TARTS

The French are famed for their pastries and especially for their fruit tarts. These have an almond flavoured cream instead of a traditional crème pâtissière filling.

Serves 4

Ingredients

Pastry

150g/5oz plain flour
60g/2oz caster sugar
½ egg yolk
2 tbsps water
Pinch of salt
60g/2oz butter, softened

Almond Cream

120g/4oz butter, softened
120g/4oz caster sugar
60g/2oz ground almonds
1 egg

Topping

225-340g/8-12oz strawberries, hulled and washed
3 tbsps strawberry glaze, or melted strawberry jam

To make the pastry, mix together the flour, sugar, egg yolk, water and salt. Add the softened butter, mix thoroughly and form into a ball. Allow to rest in the refrigerator. Make the almond cream by beating together the butter and sugar until light. Add the ground almonds and the egg, mix well and set aside in the refrigerator. Dry the strawberries. Trim as necessary and slice neatly.

Preheat the oven to 200°C/400°F/Gas Mark 6. Roll out the pastry and use to line four individual non-stick tins, or one large one (about 20cm/8 inches in diameter) if preferred. Prick the bases with a fork. Either use a piping bag to pipe the almond cream into the tart cases or simply spoon in the cream and spread it evenly with the back of the spoon. Bake in the preheated oven for 20 minutes. When the tarts are cooked, allow them to cool and then arrange the strawberries decoratively over the cream. Brush the strawberries with the glaze, leave them to set for 30 minutes in the refrigerator and serve chilled.

FRUIT SORBETS

There are two varieties of fruit sorbets, one with egg white and one without. Lighter and more refreshing than ice cream, these are excellent desserts to have in your freezer, ready for unexpected guests.

Serves 4-6

INGREDIENTS
Sorbet a l'orange
250g/9oz caster sugar
Zest of 1 orange
280ml/½ pint fresh orange juice
120ml/4fl oz fresh lemon juice

Dissolve the sugar in 570ml/1 pint water, bring to the boil and boil continuously for 10 minutes. Set aside to cool. Blanch the orange zest in boiling water, for 15 seconds. Mix the cooled syrup with the orange and lemon juice, and stir in the zest. Pour the mixture into a plastic container and place in the freezer. Remove the sorbet from the freezer every 30 minutes and beat with a fork until it has completely crystallised.

INGREDIENTS
Pear Sorbet
75g/2½oz caster sugar
460g/1lb pears, peeled and chopped
3 tbsps lemon juice
1 egg white and a pinch of salt

Dissolve the sugar in 150ml/¼ pint water, add the chopped pear, then bring to the boil and boil continuously for 10 minutes. Set aside to cool. Once cool, purée in a liquidiser or food processor until smooth. Stir in the lemon juice, then pour into a plastic container and freeze for 1 hour.

After 1 hour, remove the sorbet and beat it well with a fork. Whisk the egg white with the salt until stiff. Fold gently into the sorbet, using a metal spoon. Cover and return to the freezer until needed.

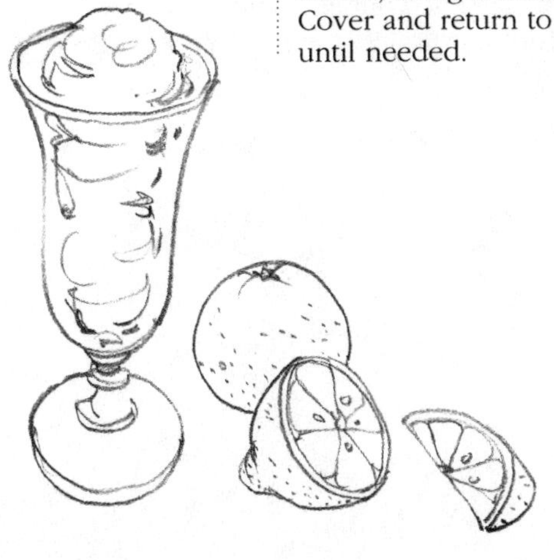

POACHED PEARS IN PORT

This is the classic way of poaching pears in red wine or port. Choose evenly sized pears with stalks – this makes them more attractive for serving.

Serves 4

INGREDIENTS
Juice of 1 lemon
4 large firm pears, peeled
570ml/1 pint port or red wine and port, mixed
1 tsp ground cinnamon
250g/9oz sugar

Pour the lemon juice over the peeled pears – this will prevent them from discolouring. Place the pears in a large saucepan, add the port and just enough water to cover. Sprinkle over the cinnamon and the sugar and cook over a gentle heat for 15-20 minutes until just cooked. Remove the pears, and either keep warm or chill in the refrigerator.

Return the juice to a brisk boil and allow it to reduce and become slightly syrupy. Pour the sauce over the pears and serve.

PROFITEROLES WITH CHOCOLATE SAUCE

I honestly don't think that you can beat home-made profiteroles for a delicious, classic dessert!

Serves 6

INGREDIENTS
Choux Pastry
280ml/½ pint water
90g/3oz butter
Pinch of salt
175g/6oz plain flour, sifted
5 large eggs, beaten

Chocolate Sauce
175g/6oz dark chocolate, melted
2 tbsps caster sugar
120ml/4fl oz whipping cream

Filling
430ml/¾ pint double cream, whipped

Preheat the oven to 220°C/425°F/Gas Mark 7. Lightly grease two baking sheets. Bring the water to the boil in a saucepan, add the butter and the pinch of salt. Boil until the butter has melted, remove the pan from the heat, and beat in the flour all at once. Beat until smooth – the pastry will form a ball and leave the sides of the pan. Gradually add the beaten egg, retaining a little for brushing, then use to fill a piping bag fitted with a plain nozzle. The pastry should be smooth and glossy and of a piping consistency.

Pipe 12 balls of choux pastry on to the baking sheets. Mix the remaining beaten egg with a little water and brush over the choux pastry balls. Cook for 10 minutes then reduce the heat to 180°C/350°F/Gas Mark 4 and cook for about 20 minutes more – the balls should double in size and be golden brown. Remove from the oven and pierce them to let the steam escape. Turn off the oven, leave the door open, and put the profiteroles back into the open oven for about 10 minutes to dry out.

Melt the chocolate and the sugar together in a bowl over a pan of boiling water, then stir in the cream. Slice open the choux buns, fill with the whipped cream. Pile up the buns in a serving dish or on a plate and pour the chocolate sauce over to serve.

TARTE AU CITRON
LEMON TART

A few lemons grow in Provençe but most of the French crop come from Corsica. This is a classic dessert from Provençe, justly popular throughout France. Here is one method of preparing Tarte au Citron.

Serves 6

INGREDIENTS

Sweet Pastry

225g/8oz plain flour, sifted
Pinch of salt
120g/4oz butter, cut into cubes
120g/4oz sugar
1 egg, beaten

Lemon Filling

120g/4oz butter
175g/6oz sugar
5 eggs, beaten
Juice of 2 lemons
Zest of ½ lemon

Preheat the oven to 190°C/375°F/Gas Mark 5. Prepare the pastry, place the flour in a mixing bowl, add the salt and rub in the butter. Stir in the sugar, then mix in the egg and form the pastry into a ball. Place in the refrigerator for 5-10 minutes. Roll out the pastry on a floured surface, and use it to line a pie tin about 20cm/8 inches in diameter. Prick the pastry base with a fork. Line the pastry case with greaseproof paper and fill with baking beans, rice or dried beans. Bake in the preheated oven for 15 minutes, then remove the beans and paper and return the patry to the oven for 5 minutes or until the pastry is firm and golden.

Mix all the ingredients for the lemon filling in a saucepan. Place over a gentle heat and stir continuously for 10 minutes. The mixture will become quite thick. Allow to cool and chill slightly in the refrigerator. Stir well and then fill the pastry shell. Keep the tart covered in the refrigerator until required.

CLAFOUTIS AUX CERISES

Clafoutis is usually made with tart, black cherries, but chopped prunes make an interesting variation. This traditional dessert is a thick sweet pancake-cum-batter pudding – delicious! Use canned cherries if necessary but drain them thoroughly before use.

Serves 8

INGREDIENTS
120g/4oz butter
570g/1¼lbs fresh cherries
225g/8oz milk
Pinch of salt
120g/4oz caster sugar
4 eggs, beaten
225g/8oz plain flour, sifted

Preheat the oven to 180°C/350°F/Gas Mark 4. Using a quarter of the butter, grease a large ovenproof dish. Spread the cherries in the bottom of the dish. Bring the milk to the boil in a saucepan, add the salt and allow to cool slightly.

Melt the remaining butter, and mix in the sugar, eggs and the flour. Pour the milk into the mixture, mix well and pour the batter over the cherries in the dish. Bake in a moderate oven for about 50 minutes. Serve warm with cream.

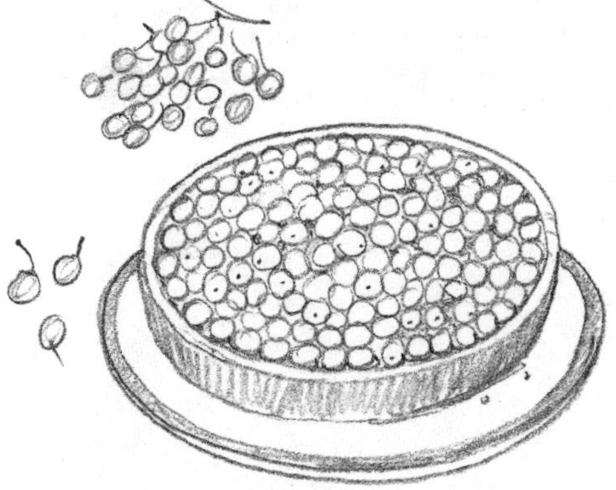

PÊCHES AU VIN ROUGE
PEACHES IN RED WINE

Peaches are one of the finest fruits grown in France, where there are many different varieties. They are delicious poached in red wine.

Serves 6

INGREDIENTS

1.14 litres/2 pints red wine
340g/12 oz sugar
280ml/½ pint water
1 stick cinnamon
1 vanilla pod
1 tbsp fresh lemon and orange zest, finely chopped
1 clove
6 firm peaches, peeled

Combine all the ingredients, except the peaches, in a large saucepan and bring to the boil. Allow to boil until the syrup has reduced somewhat and is slightly thickened. Place the peaches in the syrup and poach them until they are cooked. Cooking time will depend on the quality and size of the peaches – test with the point of a sharp knife; there should be just a little resistance when cooked.

Remove the peaches from the syrup. Allow the syrup to cool slightly and remove the clove, vanilla and the cinnamon.

Slice the peaches and spread out into fan shapes on small individual plates. Pour the syrup over and serve.

ÉCLAIRS

Éclairs are finger-shaped choux pastries. They are traditionally filled with cream or crème pâtissière and iced with chocolate, but many different fillings and toppings are used. I like coffee icing for a change.

Makes 12

Ingredients

Choux Pastry
200ml/7fl oz water
90g/3oz butter or margarine
90g/3oz plain flour, sifted
3 eggs

Filling
280ml/1/2 pint Crème pâtissière (see recipe)

Glacé Icing
460g/1lb icing sugar
Hot water
Few drops vanilla essence

Preheat the oven to 180°C/350°F/Gas Mark 4. Combine the water and butter for the pastry in a deep saucepan and bring to the boil. Once boiling rapidly, take the pan off the heat. Stir in the flour all at once and beat just until the mixture leaves the side of the pan. Spread out on to a plate to cool. When cool, return to the saucepan and gradually add the beaten eggs. Beat well in between each addition of egg until the paste is smooth and shiny – it should be of soft dropping consistency, but holding its shape well. It may not be necessary to add all the egg.

Pipe or spoon the pastry into strips about 7.5cm/3 inches long, spaced well apart on lightly-greased baking sheets. Sprinkle the sheets lightly with water and place in the oven. Immediately increase oven temperature to 190°C/375°F/Gas Mark 5. Make sure the pastry is very crisp before removing it from the oven: this will take about 20-30 minutes. If the pastry is not crisp, return it to the oven for a further 5 minutes.

Sift the icing sugar into a bowl and add hot water, stirring constantly until the mixture is of thick coating consistency. The icing should cover the back of a wooden spoon but run off slowly. Add the vanilla essence.

To assemble the éclairs, cut the choux pastry almost in half lengthways and either pipe or spoon in the Crème Pâtissière. Using a large spoon, coat the top of each eclair with a smooth layer of glacé icing. Allow the icing to set before serving.

TARTE TATIN

An upside-down apple tart, created by two sisters named Tatin who ran a restaurant in the Loire valley. One of the most popular of French desserts.

Serves 6

Ingredients
460g/1lb flaky pastry
1kg/2¼lbs apples, peeled, halved and cored
90g/3oz butter
175g/6oz sugar
Whipped cream for serving

Preheat the oven to 230°C/450°F/Gas Mark 8. Dot the base of a pie tin (about 20cm/8 inches in diameter) with the butter and sprinkle with half the sugar. Place the apple halves, rounded side down, on to the butter and sugar, and sprinkle with the remaining sugar. Roll the pastry out into a round just slightly larger than the bottom of the tin and place it over the apples, tucking it down at the edges.

Cook in a very hot oven for about 30 minutes. Remove from the oven when cooked and turn out immediately on to a serving plate. Serve hot with cream.

PRALINE MILLEFEUILLE

Pastry slices are often filled with cream and strawberries, but the praline flavoured confectioners cream or custard gives a bitter-sweet filling which I actually prefer.

Serves 4

INGREDIENTS

225ml/8fl oz milk
1 tbsp crushed Praline (see recipe)
2 egg yolks
2½ tbsps sugar
1½ tbsps flour, sieved
225g/8oz puff pastry
Icing sugar
Cocoa powder

Preheat the oven to 200°C/400°F/Gas Mark 6, and slightly dampen a baking sheet. Boil the milk with the crushed praline. Beat the egg yolks with the sugar until pale and fluffy, then beat in the flour, mixing well. Pour the hot milk over the mixture, stir well and pour back into the saucepan. Bring to the boil, then reduce the heat and cook, stirring continuously, until the mixture thickens. Set aside to cool.

Roll the pastry out very thinly into a large rectangle and place on a large baking sheet, then bake in the hot oven for 10 minutes until risen and golden. Remove from the oven and allow to cool. Carefully cut the cooked, cooled pastry first into three long strips and then crossways into 12 evenly-sized rectangles. Spread a little of the pastry cream over one of the rectangles, then cover with another piece of pastry, spread with more filling and finish with a third pastry rectangle. Continue until you have four millefeuilles. Sift a little icing sugar and cocoa over the top of the pastries to decorate.

GALETTES DE ROIS
KING'S CAKES

These cakes are traditionally served at the feast of Epiphany. A charm may be baked in the filling of one of the pastries in the same way that a charm or a coin might be hidden in a Christmas pudding.

Serves 4

INGREDIENTS

60g/2oz softened butter
4 tbsps caster sugar
1 egg, beaten
8 tbsps ground almonds
2 tbsps Crème Pâtissière (see recipe)
1 tsp rum
460g/1lb puff pastry
1 egg, beaten

Preheat the oven to 230°C/450°F/Gas Mark 8 and lightly grease a large baking sheet. Cream together the butter and sugar, then add the egg and ground almonds to give a thick almond cream. Beat in the crème pâtissière and the rum until thoroughly mixed.

Roll out the pastry thinly and cut it into eight circles, four of which should be slightly larger then the others. Place the four smaller circles on the greased baking sheet and prick them all over with a fork. Place the almond cream in a piping bag, fitted with a plain nozzle,and pipe the cream into the centre of the circles, leaving a wide margin all the way around the filling. Brush a little beaten egg around the edges of the pastry circles, then cover them with the larger circles, pressing the edges together and crimping them to seal the galettes completely. Brush the tops with the remaining beaten egg to give the cooked galettes a glossy finish. Cook in the preheated oven for about 20 minutes, until the galettes are golden brown.

FRUIT MILLEFEUILLES

Assemble the pastries at the last possible moment to keep them crisp. Use your favourite fresh fruits in season and serve the fruit slices with a slightly sharp raspberry coulis. I think the ideal size for these pastries is 10 × 6.5cm or 4 × 2½ inches – substantial but not too big.

Serves 4

Ingredients

340g/12oz puff pastry
150ml/¼ pint double cream
5 tbsps Crème Pâtissière (see recipe)
1 tsp any orange liqueur
2 kiwi fruits
5 clementines

Preheat the oven to 200°C/400°F/Gas Mark 6. Dampen two baking sheets. Roll out the pastry very thinly to fit the two dampened baking sheets. Prick all over with a fork, then bake in the preheated oven for about 10-15 minutes, until browned. Whip the cream and fold it into the pastry cream with the orange liqueur. Peel the kiwi fruits and slice them into rounds. Peel and segment the clementines, removing the skin from each segment.

Cut each cooled pastry sheet into six equal portions, making twelve in total. Divide the cream evenly between the twelve portions, spreading it smoothly. Decorate four with the clementine segments, and another four with the kiwi slices, reserving a little of each fruit for decorating the finished pastries. Top each clementine portion first with a kiwi portion and then with a plain portion. Decorate each pastry with the reserved fruit and serve.

FRENCH APPLE TURNOVERS

A classic recipe of Normandy, one of the main apple growing areas of France. Cinnamon is the traditional seasoning, but I like to use ground mace with apples occasionally for a change.

Serves 4

INGREDIENTS
460g/1lb apples
3 tbsps sugar
150ml/¼ pint water
460g/1lb puff pastry
Cinnamon
1 egg, beaten

Preheat the oven to 200°C/400°F/Gas Mark 6. Lightly grease a baking sheet. Peel, core and dice the apples. Place them in a saucepan with the sugar and water and cook, stirring occasionally, until the water has evaporated. Use a fork to mash the apples to a smooth purée, and reserve about 6 tbsps of this purée.

Roll out the pastry but not too thinly. Cut out four large circles, place on the baking sheet and prick them all over with a fork. Spoon 1½ tbsps of apple purée over one half of each of the pastry circles. Sprinkle with cinnamon to taste. Brush beaten egg around the edges of each circle. Fold each empty pastry half over the apple purée, press the edges together and crimp them with your fingers to seal well and prevent leakage during cooking. Brush the turnovers with beaten egg and bake for 20 minutes in the preheated oven until golden brown. Allow to cool slightly before serving.

PARIS-BREST

A Parisienne speciality, originally created to celebrate the Paris to Brest cycle race. Small pastries make attractive individual servings but this dessert may also be made in a large circle and sliced. The praline cream filling is essential.

Serves 4

INGREDIENTS
Choux Pastry
120ml/4fl oz water
2 tbsps butter
1 tsp sugar
Pinch of salt
4 tbsps flour
2 eggs
1 tbsp slivered almonds
Icing sugar

Filling
225ml/8fl oz double cream
4 tbsps crushed Praline (see recipe)
4 tbsps Crème Pâtissière (see recipe)

Preheat the oven to 200°C/400°F/Gas Mark 6. Lightly grease a baking sheet. Place the water, butter, sugar and salt in a saucepan and bring to the boil. When the butter has melted and the water is boiling, add the flour all at once. Beat continuously for a few minutes until the dough comes away cleanly from the sides of the pan and forms a ball. Remove the pan from the heat and beat in the eggs one by one, reserving a little for glazing, to obtain a smooth dough suitable for piping. Spoon into a forcing bag, fitted with a plain nozzle, and pipe four rings on to the greased baking sheet. Brush the pastry with the reserved beaten egg and sprinkle with the almonds. Bake for 20 minutes in the preheated oven until golden brown. Remove the choux rings from the oven, allow them to cool on a wire rack and then slice them in half horizontally.

To make the filling, whip the cream until stiff. Add the praline to the crème pâtissière, then fold in the whipped cream. Place the filling in a piping bag with a plain metal nozzle. Pipe the filling into the bottom half of the choux rings, then replace the tops. Sift icing sugar over the pastries and serve immediately.

AMANDINES

These are rich sweet tarts and may be made at any time of year. I think that they are typical winter 'comfort' food.

Serves 4

INGREDIENTS
Half quantity sweet pastry (see reicpe)
60g/2oz softened butter
4 tbsps sugar
1 egg
120g/4oz ground almonds
2 tbsps raspberry jam

Preheat the oven to 180°C/350°F/Gas Mark 4. Roll out the pastry and use it to line four individual, greased pie tins. Set aside in the refrigerator.

Beat the butter and sugar together until pale, then add the egg and continue to beat until completely mixed. Stir in the ground almonds to form a thick paste – add a little more if necessary. Spread the jam evenly over the base of the four pastry cases, and spoon the almond mixture carefully and evenly over the jam, or use a piping bag to pipe it. Do not overfill the pastry cases.

Bake the amandines in the preheated oven for about 30 minutes. Allow to cool before removing from the tins.

BASIC RECIPES

The recipes contained within this chapter may seem like a rather odd assortment and, in truth, I suppose that they are! However, they are a collection of basic recipes without which no book on Classic French Cookery would be complete!

Basic Sauces

Here are the recipes for vinaigrette and mayonnaise, two salad dressings that are common to almost every western cuisine. There are many different ways of preparing both – if you don't get the flavour and seasoning quite right the first time, persevere until the dressing is to your liking. I usually use sugar in vinaigrette but some people like to use honey – brown sugar will give a slightly richer flavour than white, and so the variations go on! I prefer to use lemon juice when making mayonnaise, others use wine vinegar. I assume that you will use Dijon mustard in the salad dressings – the yellow English mustard will work just as well but has a stronger, more pungent flavour. Aïoli, a rich garlic sauce somewhat akin to mayonnaise, is served with many French dishes and a recipe is included elsewhere in this book. An easy recipe for Hollandaise, another sauce used extensively with fish and vegetables, is included here.

Sweet Success

There are two custard recipes which everyone should have at their fingertips in order to prepare a really diverse and successful range of sweet dishes. One is Crème Pâtissière, a rich, thick vanilla custard which is often used in place of cream as a filling for tarts and pastries, and the other is an egg custard sauce. This bears no relationship at all to instant custard! In the new style of French cuisine, nouvelle cuisine, egg custard sauce is often served under tartlets or poached fruits, so as not to mask their appearance. Chocolate sauce or redcurrant jelly may be marbled through the sauce for extra effect.

Egg Dishes for Light Lunches or Suppers

I have also included several egg dishes in this section, simply because they didn't seem to belong anywhere else! Piperade is almost a Spanish Omelette, whereas the Scrambled Eggs with Olives recipe belongs to the new style of French cookery, a development which is keeping the traditional cuisine alive. I have also included a recipe for Quiche Lorraine. Was there ever a dish that was so plagiarised and plundered? The original recipe hails from Alsace-Lorraine and should include bacon cooked in an egg custard within a pastry case. Quiche should never be eaten hot – cutting the flan when it comes straight from the oven makes the filling separate and become watery – always serve quiche warm or cold. If you must add vegetables to the filling, cook them lightly and drain off any juices that may come from them during cooking – these would make the pastry soggy and may cause the filling to curdle.

Sweet, Short Biscuits

The French are very good biscuit makers and even their commercially baked biscuits are really quite special. There are three different biscuits that are often served with coffee or with sorbets, mousses and other desserts; *tuilles almandes*, *langues de chats* and *palmiers*, all named because of their distinctive shapes. Even French commercial biscuits cannot compare in flavour to those made at home! They are all quite simple to make and to bake – shaping the *tuilles almandes* is the most complicated process, but a good supply of pencils will help with that. When shaping biscuits, move quickly – they have to be moulded straight from the oven, or they will harden and set. Should that happen before you have shaped them, put the biscuits back into the oven for just a couple of minutes on their baking sheet to soften again – no harm will come to them.

Cakes in France are often lighter than traditional cakes baked elsewhere. A sponge cake in the U.K. would generally refer to a Victoria Sandwich mixture, whereas in France it would be a whisked sponge. Fruit cakes are lighter as well, and are usually baked in tranche or loaf tins. I have simply run out of space, even in a collection of 200 recipes, to include much baking, but I have managed to squeeze in a *Gâteau Breton*, a Breton Butter Cake, which is almost a cross between a rich pastry and a biscuit. It is delicious by itself but is equally good served with fruit mousses and desserts, in a similar way to fingers of shortbread. Make sure that you use good unsalted butter for this recipe.

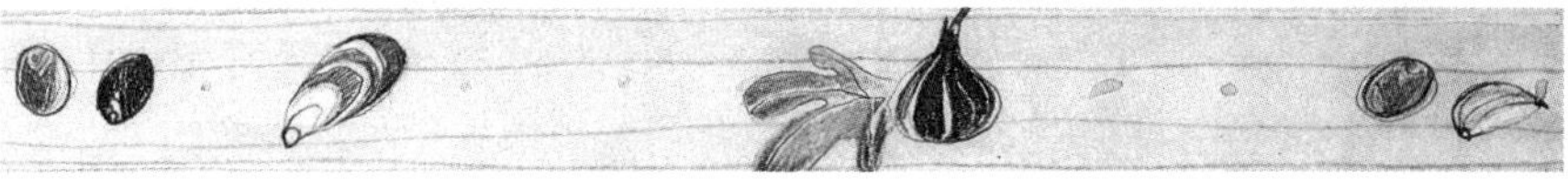

VINAIGRETTE OR FRENCH DRESSING

This dressing is used in so many different ways, as a salad dressing, hot over vegetables and as a seasoning. There are many recipes but this is the way I like to make it, using the best of French ingredients.

Serves 4

INGREDIENTS
6 tbsps extra virgin olive oil
2 tbsps good wine vinegar
Salt and freshly ground black pepper
1 tsp Dijon mustard, or more to taste
Pinch of sugar
Freshly chopped mixed herbs or crushed garlic

Place all the ingredients in a screw-topped jar or vinaigrette shaker and shake until well blended. Taste carefully and season as required. Herbs or garlic may be added for extra flavour. Use as required.

MAYONNAISE

This is probably the *classic cold sauce in international cuisine. It is based on eggs and oil, so it is rich in flavour and calories! I actually don't like to use olive oil in mayonnaise – I find the flavour too strong, and prefer to use a sunflower or safflower oil.*

Makes about 280ml/½ pint

Ingredients

3 egg yolks, or 1 whole egg plus one yolk
½ tsp dry mustard
Salt and white pepper
1 tbsp wine vinegar or lemon juice
Pinch of sugar
280ml/½ pint sunflower oil

Place all the ingredients except the oil in a liquidiser or food processor and blend together briefly. Add the oil in a steady stream, with the machine running, and listen for the mayonnaise to thicken – it will sound deeper!

Season to taste and use as required.

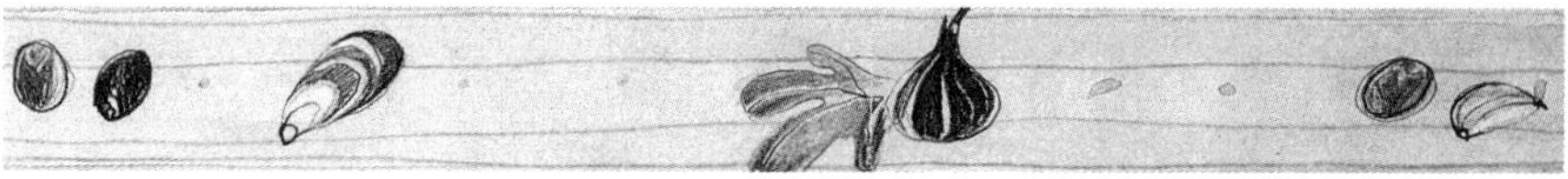

QUICK HOLLANDAISE SAUCE

An easy way to produce a classic buttery sauce. This is excellent to serve with fish or vegetables.

INGREDIENTS
175g/6oz butter
1 tbsp wine or tarragon vinegar
2 tbsps lemon juice
3 egg yolks
½ tsp caster sugar
Pinch of salt
Pinch of cayenne pepper (optional)

Melt the butter slowly in a small saucepan and, in another, heat the vinegar and lemon juice to boiling point. Put the egg yolks, sugar, salt and cayenne in a blender and process for a few seconds. With the machine still running, very gradually add the vinegar and lemon juice mixture. When the butter has reached the boil, add this to the egg mixture in a slow drizzle, also with the machine running, until it is all incorporated and the sauce has thickened.

Serve at once or keep warm by transferring it to a bowl placed over a saucepan of hot water.

SCRAMBLED EGGS WITH OLIVES

The addition of black olives to scrambled eggs turns this simple dish into a memorable one.

Serves 4

INGREDIENTS
12 eggs
4 tomatoes, seeded and chopped
15 black olives, pitted
120ml/4fl oz olive oil
1 small onion, chopped
1 clove garlic, chopped
30g/1oz butter
Salt and freshly ground black pepper

Beat the eggs and set them aside. Chop the tomatoes and the olives together finely using a liquidiser or food processor. Warm the olive oil in a frying pan, increase the heat to high and cook the onion, garlic, tomatoes and olives until all the juices have evaporated.

Melt the butter in a large saucepan, add the beaten egg and cook over a gentle heat, stirring continuously with a wooden spoon. Once the eggs are cooked, stir in the tomato mixture and season to taste. Serve on small, pre-warmed plates.

OMELETTES GOURMANDES

Omelette making is an art and, of course, the French are particularly good at it. Serve this large omelette sliced.

Serves 4

INGREDIENTS
4 onions, finely chopped
5 tbsps oil
120g/4oz mushrooms
12 eggs, beaten
1 tbsp freshly chopped herbs
Salt and freshly ground black pepper

Sauté the onions in 2 tbsps of oil over a high heat, then reduce the heat and cook for a further 20 minutes, until softened and lightly caramelised. In another large frying pan, sauté the mushrooms in 1 tablespoon of the oil until soft. Remove from the heat. Add the beaten eggs to the mushrooms, stir in half the onions, and cook over a high heat in as much of the remaining oil as necessary. Sprinkle with the herbs and cook the omelette until the base is crisp but the filling is still slightly liquid. Fold one side of the omelette into the middle, then fold over the other side.

Serve on a bed of the remaining onions with a little salt and pepper. Serve sliced.

CHEESE SOUFFLÉ

Soufflés are popular throughout France. Many people worry about preparing hot soufflés as they do collapse soon after cooking, so have everyone ready for the moment that the soufflé comes out of the oven.

Serves 6

INGREDIENTS
Butter for greasing
175g/6oz grated cheese
30g/1oz butter
30g/1oz plain flour
280ml/½ pint milk
Salt and freshly ground black pepper
Pinch of nutmeg
4 eggs, separated
1 extra egg white

Preheat the oven to 190°C/375°F/Gas Mark 5. Grease a soufflé dish with butter and scatter 3 tbsps of the grated cheese inside it. Melt the butter in a heavy saucepan, whisk in the flour, cook for about 1 minute, then gradually add the milk and whisk continuously until the mixture thickens. Reduce the heat and cook for 2 minutes. Add the salt and pepper, nutmeg and the egg yolks one by one, beating well with a wooden spoon. Leave to cool for about 5 minutes. Stir the remaining cheese into the white sauce. Whisk the 5 egg whites until firm, then fold them gently into the cheese mixture with a metal spoon. Pour the mixture into the prepared soufflé dish and cook in a hot oven for 40-45 minutes. The soufflé should be well risen and golden. Serve immediately.

QUICHE LORRAINE

The classic dish from the Lorraine region of France, in the north east of the country. I once found a postcard of a quiche with a completely burnt, black top to the filling – don't let yours overcook!

Serves 6-8

INGREDIENTS

Pastry

175g/6oz plain flour
90g/3oz butter
Pinch of salt
½ egg, beaten with 1 tbsp water

Filling

3 thick rashers bacon, diced
4 eggs, beaten
120ml/4fl oz milk
175ml/6fl oz double cream
Pinch of grated nutmeg
Salt and freshly ground black pepper

Preheat the oven to 190°C/375°F/Gas Mark 5. To make the pastry, rub the butter into the flour with your fingertips until the mixture resembles fine breadcrumbs. Add the salt and bind the mixture together with the beaten egg and a little cold water. Place in the refrigerator for 5 minutes to rest.

Roll out the pastry and use it to line a pie dish 17.5-20cm/7-8 inches in diameter. Dot the base of the pie with the diced bacon. Beat together the eggs, milk, cream, nutmeg and a little salt and pepper. Pour the egg mixture into the flan and cook immediately in the oven for 35-40 minutes. Serve warm or cold.

PISSALADIÈRE

You could describe this wonderful dish as a French pizza! The topping is a rich mixture of caramelised onions with thyme, anchovies and olives, cooked in the best traditions of Provençe, from where the recipe originates.

Serves 6

INGREDIENTS

1.14kg/2lbs onions
8tbsps extra virgin olive oil
2 fat cloves garlic, finely sliced
6 or 7 sprigs thyme
Salt and freshly ground black pepper
2 bay leaves
460g/1lb strong white bread flour
1 tsp sea salt
30g/1oz fresh yeast
15g/½oz sugar
60g/2oz can anchovy fillets in olive oil, drained
Black olives for garnish

Peel and finely slice the onions. Heat 3 tbsps of olive oil in a large frying pan, add the onions and cook for 5 minutes, stirring once or twice. When the onions have started to go down in volume add the sliced garlic, salt and pepper, thyme and bay leaves. Cover and cook slowly for about 2 hours, until the onions have caramelised and cooked almost to a paste. Turn the onions into a sieve over a measuring jug and allow the juice to drain into the jug.

Place the flour and sea salt together in a bowl and make a well in the centre. Add the remaining olive oil. Cream the yeast with the sugar. Measure the warm onion liquid and make it up to 225ml/8fl oz with water, adding a little to the yeast. Add the yeast and onion juice to the flour and mix to a soft manageable dough. Knead on a lightly floured work surface until smooth. Place the dough in a large mixing bowl and cover. Leave in a warm place for 1 hour, until the dough has doubled in size.

Scrape the dough from the bowl and knead it lightly again. Roll out to a rectangle to fit a large rectangular, lightly oiled baking tray. Pull the dough to shape to fit into the corners. Leave, covered, for a further 20 minutes to prove again.

Preheat the oven to 220°C/425°F/Gas Mark 7. Brush the dough with a little olive oil then spread it with the onion mixture, removing the thyme and bay leaves. Season with salt and pepper and arrange the anchovy fillets and olives over the Pissaladière. Drizzle with extra olive oil.

Bake in the preheated oven for 15-20 minutes. Cut into slices and serve immediately.

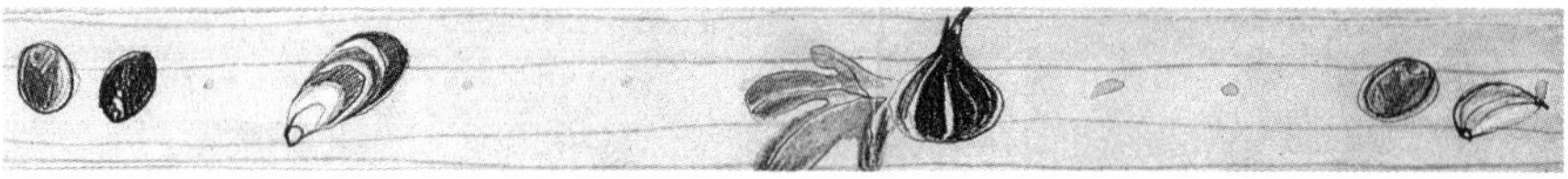

TARTE DE PROVENÇE

A richly flavoured tart that is ideal for summer eating. Serve warm or cold – this is excellent picnic food.

Serves 6

INGREDIENTS

Pastry

120g/4oz self raising flour
60g/2oz butter and white cooking fat, mixed
Cold water

Filling

460g/1lb ripe tomatoes
1 medium onion
15g/½oz butter
Pinch of mixed herbs
2 tbsps tomato purée
2 eggs, beaten
120g/4oz grated cheese
Salt and freshly ground black pepper
60g/2oz can anchovy fillets
Black olives

Preheat the oven to 190°C/375°F/Gas Mark 5. Prepare the pastry by rubbing the fat into the flour and salt until the mixture resembles fine breadcrumbs. Mix to a firm dough with cold water. Roll out and use to line a 20cm/8 inch quiche tin or porcelain flan dish. Chill until required.

Plunge the tomatoes into boiling water for a few seconds, remove and peel off the skins. Halve the tomatoes and remove the seeds and cores. Chop the remaining flesh. Peel and finely chop the onion. Melt the butter in a large saucepan and add the tomatoes, onion, herbs and tomato purée. Cover and cook gently for 30 minutes until the mixture is reduced to a rich pulp. Take off the heat and allow to cool for a minute or so and then beat in the eggs, cheese and seasoning. Pour this mixture into the prepared flan case, decorate with a lattice of anchovy fillets and dot with halved, pitted black olives. Bake above the centre of the oven for 40 minutes until risen. (Always place a porcelain or china dish on a preheated baking tray to conduct the heat and ensure that the underneath of the pastry is well cooked.) Serve warm or cold.

PIPÉRADE

A dish from the Pyrenees, an omelette showing Spanish influence in its use of peppers and tomatoes. Some people add tomato purée, others slices of Jambon de Bayonne (Bayonne ham). Do not over-cook the omelette – it will toughen the egg and spoil the dish.

Serves 2–4

INGREDIENTS
- 4 eggs
- Salt and freshly ground black pepper
- 1 tbsp freshly chopped marjoram and thyme
- 1 tbsp olive oil
- 1 medium onion, chopped
- 1 medium green pepper, seeded and chopped
- 1 clove garlic, crushed
- 2 tomatoes, skinned, seeded and sliced
- 30g/1oz butter

Crack the eggs into a bowl and beat thoroughly with the salt and pepper and herbs.

Heat the oil in a frying pan and add the chopped onion, green pepper and garlic. Fry gently until soft but not brown. Add the tomatoes and cook for a further 3 minutes. Remove from the heat and add to the egg mixture.

Heat the butter in the frying pan and, when frothing, add the omelette mixture. Cook gently until the underside is golden brown. Slide out onto a plate and return to the frying pan on the reverse side. Cook for a minute or two more. Do not over cook.

Serve hot immediately or allow to cool completely and cut into wedges for a picnic or cold buffet.

CARAMEL

This is a basic recipe for use in so many sweets and desserts. Sometimes quantities of sugar and water will be given in an individual recipe but the basic method of making a caramel is always the same.

INGREDIENTS
175g/6oz granulated or caster sugar
4 tbsps cold water

Place the sugar and water in a small saucepan and heat very gently until the sugar is dissolved – you do not want the mixture to boil until the sugar has dissolved. Stir well.

Bring the mixture to the boil and boil rapidly until the caramel is a light golden colour – do not stir while the caramel is boiling. Use immediately, or plunge the base of the pan into cold water to prevent the caramel from cooking on and burning. Use quickly.

PRALINE

Praline is a nutty caramel, usually left to harden and then crushed or ground before use. It is most commonly made with hazelnuts or almonds. The nuts are usually left in their skins for extra colour, but may be blanched if preferred.

INGREDIENTS

120g/4oz hazelnuts or almonds, toasted if wished

175g/6oz granulated or caster sugar

4 tbsps cold water

Roughly chop the nuts and place them on a thick, lightly greased baking sheet. Place the sugar and water in a small saucepan and heat very gently until the sugar is dissolved – you do not want the mixture to boil until the sugar has dissolved. Stir well.

Bring the mixture to the boil and boil rapidly until the caramel is a light golden colour – do not stir while the caramel is boiling. Pour over the nuts and leave to set until hard.

Crush the praline into small pieces – this is easiest to do with the end of a rolling pin. The praline may be ground finely in a pestle and mortar. Use as required.

EGG CUSTARD SAUCE

A classic vanilla flavoured sauce. It is used to pour over desserts or, in a more stylish cuisine, is often served under food, as a bed of sauce. For special occasions make the custard with double cream!

Serves 4

6 egg yolks
2 tbsps caster sugar
1 tsp cornflour
570ml/1pint milk
Few drops vanilla essence

Whisk the egg yolks, sugar and cornflour together lightly. Bring the milk almost to the boil, then pour it onto the egg mixture, whisking constantly. Rinse the pan.

Return the custard to the pan and heat very gently, stirring all the time, until the sauce starts to thicken and will coat the back of a wooden spoon. Use as required.

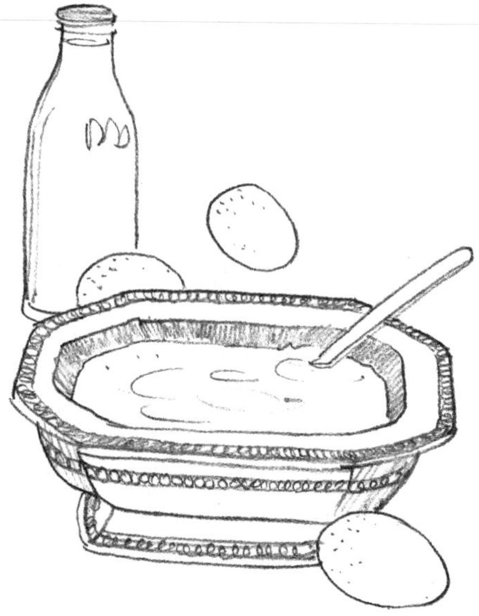

CRÈME PÂTISSIÈRE

This recipe will make just over 280ml/½ pint of crème pâtissière or confectioners custard. I often use this as a filling for fruit tarts – it is creamy but not too rich.

INGREDIENTS
280ml/½ pint milk
Vanilla pod or a few drops vanilla essence
3 egg yolks
60g/2oz caster sugar
2 tbsps cornflour
15g/½oz butter

Pour the milk into a saucepan and add the vanilla pod. Bring to the boil then remove from the heat and leave for about 20 minutes to infuse. Whisk together the egg yolks, sugar and cornflour until thick and creamy. Add vanilla essence at this stage if you have not used a vanilla pod. Remove the pod from the milk and slowly pour the liquid over the egg yolk mixture, stirring continuously. Rinse out the saucepan and return the mixture to it. Stir vigorously over a low heat until the custard becomes thick. Transfer it to a bowl and beat in the butter. Allow to cool. Cover with plastic wrap or greaseproof paper until needed. The crème pâtissière can be flavoured with a little liqueur or lightened by the addition of whipped cream.

SWEET PASTRY

This is a classic pastry used for many sweet dishes and flans – it is often called a pâté sablé. It is richer than shortcrust pastry and is made with self-raising flour. The pastry should be baked in an oven no hotter than 190°C/375°F/Gas Mark 5, because of the high proportion of sugar which will cause the pastry to brown quickly.

INGREDIENTS
460g/1lb self-raising flour
150g/5oz butter
150g/5oz caster sugar
3 eggs, beaten

Place the flour in a large bowl and add the butter, then rub in the butter until the mixture resembles fine breadcrumbs. Stir in the sugar, then add the beaten eggs and bind the pastry together using your hands.

Knead gently on a lightly floured surface, then wrap in plastic wrap or foil and chill until required.

PALMIERS

Palmiers are sweet, crisp pastry biscuits, deriving their shape from a process whereby the ends of the pastry are rolled towards the centre forming attractive double curls. These biscuits are best served on the day that they are made. Use caster sugar or icing sugar to dredge the biscuits.

Serves 4-6

INGREDIENTS
225g/8oz puff pastry
3 tbsps caster sugar plus sugar for dredging

Preheat the oven to 200°C/400°F/Gas Mark 6. Lightly grease a baking sheet. Roll the pastry out to form a thin rectangle. Sprinkle the work surface with half the sugar, and place the dough on the sugared surface, then sprinkle it with the remaining sugar. Lightly press the pastry so that the sugar sticks to it. Roll the two ends of the pastry towards the middle, and place the rolled dough in the freezer for 20 minutes, to make it easier to slice.

Remove the pastry from the freezer and slice it thinly to form the curled biscuits. Place them on a dampened baking sheet, and bake in the preheated oven for 20 minutes, or until golden brown. Allow the biscuits to cool, then sprinkle them with extra sugar before serving.

TUILLES ALMANDES
ALMOND TILE BISCUITS

These almond biscuits are the perfect accompaniment to ice creams and mousses. Larger biscuits should be moulded over a rolling pin whilst smaller biscuits can be shaped over wooden pencils. They are named after the curved terracotta roof tiles popular throughout France.

Makes 30 biscuits

INGREDIENTS
120g/4oz sugar
2 egg whites
60g/2oz plain flour
60g/2oz butter, melted
90g/3oz ground almonds
Extra butter for greasing

Preheat the oven to 200°C/400°F/Gas Mark 6. Lightly grease some baking trays. Beat the sugar into the egg whites, then add the flour and butter, beating well. Beat in the almonds, then allow the mixture to rest for 10 minutes.

Place spoonfuls of mixture onto the prepared baking sheets, allowing space for the biscuits to spread, and bake each tray for 3-4 minutes. Remove the biscuits from the trays with a spatula and immediately shape them around a wooden pencil. They will cool and harden very quickly. Slide on to a wire rack to cool. Repeat the cooking and cooling operation until all the biscuit batter has been used.

LANGUES DE CHAT

No shop-bought langues de chat can ever compare in flavour to the home-made biscuits. Use a 1.25cm/½ inch nozzle to pipe the biscuits on to the baking sheets, and store the cooked biscuits in an airtight tin.

Serves 6

INGREDIENTS
150g/5oz butter, softened
460g/1lb caster sugar
½ tsp vanilla essence
5 egg whites
225g/8oz plain flour, sieved

Preheat the oven to 220°C/425°F/Gas Mark 7. Lightly grease two baking sheets. Cream the butter and sugar until pale and fluffy, then add the vanilla essence. Add the egg whites one by one, alternating with the flour, until a fine dough is obtained.

Place the dough in a piping bag with a plain nozzle and pipe evenly-sized strips of mixture onto the greased baking sheets. Leave space between the biscuits as they spread during baking. Bake in the preheated oven for 10-15 minutes: the edges of the biscuits should be golden brown but the centres still pale.

Allow the biscuits to cool slightly on the baking sheet, then use a palette knife to lift them on to a wire rack to cool completely.

GÂTEAU BRETON
BRETON BUTTER CAKE

This rich, buttery cake is a cross between a shortbread, a sponge cake and a rich pastry. Serve with a fruit pudding or eat it by itself.

Serves 8

Ingredients
6 egg yolks
200g/7oz unsalted butter, at room temperature
175g/6oz caster sugar
250g/9oz plain flour

Preheat the oven to 160°C/325°F/Gas Mark 3. Beat the egg yolks together in a bowl, then reserve a little of the egg in a small container. Add the softened butter to the egg yolks and beat until soft and well blended. Add the sugar and flour and work into a slightly sticky dough.

Lightly butter a 22.5cm/9 inch loose-bottomed cake tin. Press the butter cake into the tin, smoothing the top with a palette knife. Score into diamonds across the top with a fork then brush with the reserved egg yolk. Bake in the preheated oven for 50 minutes. Cool slightly before transferring to a wire rack.

PETS DE NONNE

These little pastry balls are slightly sweet and very crisp. Serve immediately after cooking, tossed in icing sugar and cinnamon, with strong coffee or tea, as a mid morning or afternoon snack.

INGREDIENTS

150ml/¼ pint water
2 tbsps butter
Pinch of salt
1 tsp caster sugar
4 tbsps plain flour
2 eggs, beaten
Oil for deep-frying
Icing sugar and cinnamon

Bring the water to the boil in a saucepan with the butter, salt and sugar. When the water is boiling, add all the flour at once and beat the mixture vigorously. Continue to beat for 1 minute over a low heat. Remove the saucepan from the heat and beat in the first egg. When this is completely incorporated, beat in the second egg to obtain a smooth, elastic dough.

Heat the oil for deep-frying in a deep pan. Place the dough in a forcing bag fitted with a plain metal nozzle. When the oil is hot, about 190°C/375°F, pipe small balls of pastry on to a palette knife, dipped in the hot oil, then use a second palette knife to slide the balls off into the hot oil. Turn the pets de nonne during cooking, so that they cook evenly all over. Cook until puffed and golden brown. Using a slotted spoon, remove the pets de nonne, drain on absorbent kitchen paper and serve them immediately, sprinkled with sifted icing sugar and cinnamon.

INDEX